THE WISDOM
OF THE
TAROT

The Wisdom of The Tarot

For the person who understands them, these cards are a wonderful means of acquiring *self-knowledge.*

The nature of these cards is such that they can produce a strong awakening affect on man's unconscious. He need only examine them one by one; in order to understand them better, read the relevant description. When he reaches the card corresponding to his inner state, his interest will suddenly be roused and the knowledge that he finds himself at the level of consciousness of that particular card will hit him like an electric shock. This card he will understand completely, find full of life and meaning, and in the depths of his being he will feel a strong response.

That these cards help us to awaken our unconscious to consciousness so that we acquire self-knowledge—a thorough understanding of ourselves—can be testified by anyone who has picked them up and examined them one by one. They are like a spiritual mirror in which we can not only recognize but also thoroughly examine and study ourselves. We realize that in a strange way certain cards correspond exactly to our inner state, and at the same time also to our state in relation to the world. We suddenly understand ourselves and our destiny...

Of course the inner states are an inherent part of us even when we do not pick up the cards. But they enable us to gain clear insight into our life and to solve our problems more easily and speedily.

Thus the spiritual powers of these strange cards begin to take effect in man and his effect is enhanced in proportion to his improved understanding of the cards. The stronger their effect on him, the greater his awareness of his soul. Thus the tarot brings man ever closer to his great goal, which is to know himself, *to be himself.*

Included in *Wisdom of the Tarot* are tarot cards specially designed for individual study and meditation.

1 LE BATELEVR

2   LA PAPESSE

3 L'IMPÉRATRICE ⅄

4   L'EMPEREVR   7

5 LE PAPE 7

L'AMOVREVX

7 LE CHARIOT

8 LA IVSTICE ᒣ

9 L'ERMITE

10 LA ROVE Dє FORTVNE ▷

12   LE PENDV

14 LA TEMPERANCE ☽

15   LE DIABLE

17   LES ETOILES

19　LE SOLEIL　ア

LE FOV

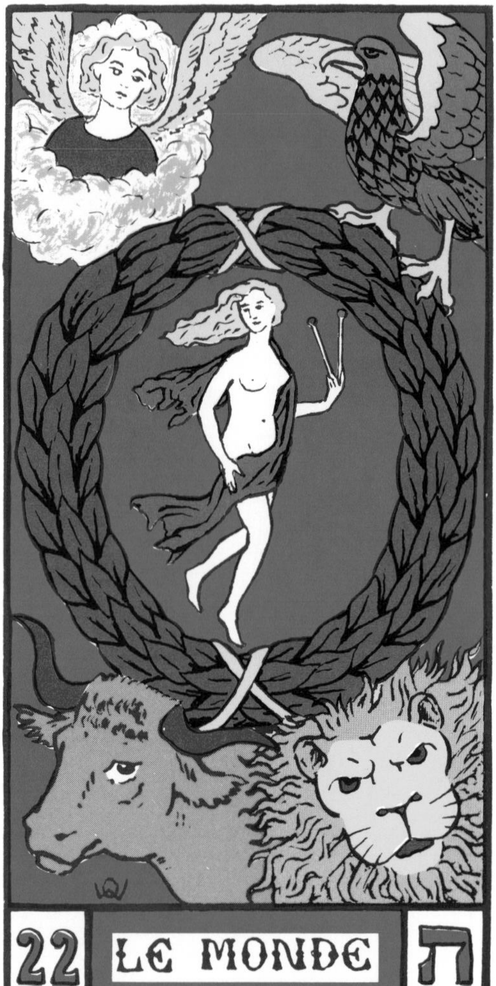
22
LE MONDE
ת

THE WISDOM
OF THE
TAROT

ALSO BY ELIZABETH HAICH

INITIATION
Seed Center Publications
SEXUAL ENERGY AND YOGA
Aurora Press
THE DAY WITH YOGA
Aurora Press
YOGA AND DESTINY
Aurora Press

THE WISDOM
OF THE
TAROT

Elisabeth Haich

Translated by D. Q. Stephenson

AURORA PRESS

P.O. Box 573   Santa Fe, N.M. 87504

First published in 1984 by
Aurora Press, Inc.
P.O. Box 573
Santa Fe, N.M. 87504

Library of Congress Cataloging in Publication Data

© Haich, Elisabeth.
   The wisdom of the tarot.

   Translation of Tarot.
   1. Tarot   I. Title
BF1879.T2H3313   1975   133.3'2424   75-22379
ISBN: 0-943358-01-9

Foreword

Paeans of acclaim greet this book on tarot.

It is written out of a full awareness of life, with a profound imaginative insight which sees the ever-renewing pattern of immediate experience – a rose, a tree in blossom, a bird – with such a sense of vitality, such all-embracing penetration, and plumbs the soul so deeply that the experiencing mind catches the eternal in what is transient and grasps within the configurations of space the presence of some moulding force transcending all spatial bounds. And it teaches us how to engage more closely with life in all its plenitude and to confront it squarely in all its tangible variety. We are shown stage by stage how to exercise our powers of pictorial thinking and ability to interpret symbols until a felicitous disposition of the cards brings the soul to intuitive knowledge of itself.

The spirit speaking to us from these ancient cards is rooted in the remote past of Egyptian mysticism. And every soul which brings these cards to life again can catch in the unchanging mirror of human life the faint intimations of an ancient past stirring in the eternally present. Thus it was once and ever will be – this image of the bonds and linkages between what appears to us to have been, to be now, and still be to come. That which is so intimately compounded in the depths is separated out in the processes of life. Starting from the beginning ever and again, it is the individual, depending on his own knowledge and his own courage, that must find his way through the labyrinth of his destiny woven from his own peculiar intrications of past, present and future. In these pages he will find the clue of Ariadne.

The keyword is integration: to become whole, to become sound, to become one – and that means: to make whole, to make sound, to unite, for only in this way can one become so oneself. Through the symbols recognised and mediated as we contemplate the correspondences between man and his destiny, the tarot pack affords us a profounder experience and a more total interiorisation of life, which speaks to us in symbols and demands from us an active response. This is achieved through the agency of the artist's eye which sees here with such clarity and truth, through the communication of a religious and ethical inspiration, and through the careful pedagogic representation which leads us upwards step by step.

To experience symbols and to be affected by them is one and the same thing. It means to be moved and uplifted in the depths of one's humanity. Their call causes man to be infused with a power stemming from the highest centres of the human spirit and also from that surpassing spirit which serves every creature and every man although existing above the level of conscious experience. Symbols renew man's creative power if he finds (and this book shows him the way) the right response to them in his inner self. For they are creative centres of energy of the spiritual power that pervades all life but is inherent in man. The man who has no answer to return to the urgent questions of the sphinx within himself falls into the abyss of the subconscious.

With all the lucidity of her artistic and creative gifts the author reveals to us with the aid of each of the twenty-two cards the corresponding levels of consciousness in man. The tarot cards, as she interprets them, are a mirror in which seeking man can see himself or someone close to him and can determine his – or their – position on the ladder of development to true man. The wisdom of Ezekiel, which is also the wisdom of Origen, calls for a whole, a true man, he who is united with the genius of humanity within himself, with his eternal self – as distinct from the merely naturally born – a divinely born 'homo humanus'. We men are all born 'men' but we do not all become 'homines humani', potentiated men, as it were, unless we are good and pious, says Origen. True man united with external and corporeal man forms the 'homo humanus' when God's image is renewed or restored in man.

It is to this knowledge and integration that the tarot pack leads us when properly understood. The language of our tarot interpretation is simple and has the dynamic *timbre* of the author's Hungarian mother tongue in which the illustrations are of such primal purity and naturalness that people of all ages and degrees of maturity, beginners as well as the more experienced, can be helped along their path. Wherever the individual may have halted on the path to unification with his genius, he will find that reading symbols so deftly presented, allowing these symbols to elicit their effect during quiet contemplation, and then following their stirrings in his inner self until the soul brings forth from its silent depths its own words and images – this, he will find, releases vital forces.

The soul thinks in images. The soul lives in images. The soul nourishes itself on the flux of images. The soul and its images are fed from the very beginning with the experiences of mankind. Conceptual thought cannot seize hold of the images now rising from the profundity of the soul with their deeply moving and gladdening effects. Intuition experiences and recognises in the bright pictures of allegory what has been experienced by the inner light. Thus in these pages the reader traverses the many fields of life. The symbolism of the sounds, rhythms, colours and forms of life is disclosed to us, the realm of the elements, the realm of the rocks, plants, and animals is revealed, the realm of man and his situation is made apparent. Thus the ancient soul of humanity speaks through the mouth of the modern spirit and shows itself to be eternally youthful, ever standing on the threshold of new miracles, always living again in the inexhaustibility of its warmth in which all creatures are lapped.

The soul of humanity, like the soul of the individual, lives only through love. Inspirited life is never immobilised in the barren monotony of mechanism. Ever and again it brings fresh animation, winged by some spirit on whose pinions it bears a kindred and loving life to all it meets.

And so this book also touches hidden depths of the soul and

wakes in them life which would otherwise sleep on, lost in the unconscious. It opens space within us and elements of the soul flow in upon us which in previous generations were accessible only to a few individuals. Through the pictures we can thus break through into a region of being which draws us into itself and nourishes and charges us with its forces. For by concentrating on an object the subject becomes pervious to the energies of the object; the subject comes into sympathetic vibration with the object and thus with the region from which the object comes.

In all ages there have been torch-bearers who through their own creative power have embodied in themselves the truth of old human wisdoms. Thus in a time of spiritual inanition dominated by the intellect the tarot pack has been made available to us again. Languages have changed but the pictures remain. With these attractive tarot cards and the author's profound and yet readily understandable interpretation, Elisabeth Haich has produced a masterly work of initiation into the secrets of life. Out of a deep understanding of being and her own intimate experience of union with her genius, she has illustrated the process by which man becomes man by his insight into the pictures of the twenty-two rungs of the ladder of divine ascent, on which each rung is an experience for the next rung in accordance with the individual's plan of life.

May this work find its way into the world and bring light and help to many.

Dr Ewalt Kliemke

Contents

Introduction

With the ever-increasing demand for the psychological interpretation of these cards, I felt impelled to publish in book form
the interpretation of the Greater Arcana of the tarot pack, in
the hope that this marvellous instrument will help men in the
immense task of acquiring self-knowledge. I therefore had to
select from the numerous tarot cards those which best served
to illustrate my explanations. Unfortunately, the tarot cards
have been frequently redesigned by people who were totally
unaware of their inner symbolic significance. Naturally, such
ignorance has led to complete falsification of this inner meaning. Although these corrupt cards may be adequate for the purpose of fortune-telling, they do not serve to represent the various
spiritual states of man. The only tarot which undoubtedly
descends from a genuine initiate, and which serves our
purpose perfectly, is the one designed and coloured by Oswald
Wirth at the dictation of the young initiate, Stanislas de Guaita,
departed before his time. These cards combine in equal measure
artistic beauty with correct symbolic depiction of their deeper
meaning. We are going to interpret these tarot cards from a
psychological angle. The cards depict the levels of human
consciousness from the first dawn of consciousness, the first
awakening, up to divine ALL-CONSCIOUSNESS, to UNION WITH
GOD.

At this point may I extend my warmest thanks to some of my
friends who have given valuable assistance with the linguistic
revision of the text.

The Wisdom of The Tarot

For the person who understands them, these cards are a wonderful means of acquiring *self-knowledge.*

The nature of these cards is such that they can produce a strong awakening affect on man's unconscious. He need only examine them one by one; in order to understand them better, read the relevant description. When he reaches the card corresponding to his inner state, his interest will suddenly be roused and the knowledge that he finds himself at the level of consciousness of that particular card will hit him like an electric shock. This card he will understand completely, find full of life and meaning, and in the depths of his being he will feel a strong response.

That these cards help us to awaken our unconscious to consciousness so that we acquire self-knowledge—a thorough understanding of ourselves—can be testified by anyone who has picked them up and examined them one by one. They are like a spiritual mirror in which we can not only recognize but also thoroughly examine and study ourselves. We realize that in a strange way certain cards correspond exactly to our inner state, and at the same time also to our state in relation to the world. We suddenly understand ourselves and our destiny...

Of course the inner states are an inherent part of us even when we do not pick up the cards. But they enable us to gain clear insight into our life and to solve our problems more easily and speedily.

Thus the spiritual powers of these strange cards begin to take effect in man and his effect is enhanced in proportion to his improved understanding of the cards. The stronger their effect on him, the greater his awareness of his soul. Thus the tarot brings man ever closer to his great goal, which is to know himself, *to be himself.*

Included in *Wisdom of the Tarot* are tarot cards specially designed for individual study and meditation.

WHAT IS 'TAROT'?

Man is like a mosaic.

The mosaic consists of a large number of small, variously coloured stones which have been arranged according to a certain pattern resulting in a beautiful, coherent picture. In the same way, man is made up of many different qualities, abilities and talents, arranged according to a specific inner pattern resulting in a coherent picture, an individual personality.

Just as the artist, using the same stones in an infinite variety of patterns, can compose all kinds of pictures in countless variations, so men also are created from the same qualities, abilities and talents, according to an infinite number and variety of inner patterns in countless variations, i.e. an infinite variety of individuals. What kind of picture emerges from an artist's hand depends entirely upon the pattern selected; that is to say, the way in which he relates the given stones to one another. Thus he can create the most varied pictures according to *whom* the picture is for, *where* it will be hung, *what effects* it should achieve and *what type of person* it should please. He can employ the same stones to create religious pictures intended to stir up feelings of devotion, for use in churches, cemeteries or other sacred places, or he can design allegorical-symbolic pictures for academic institutions such as schools, universities or libraries. Again, the artist can produce humorous, cheerful pictures for places of entertainment such as theatres or ball-rooms, or he can even create titillating and obscene pictures for the haunts of the demi-monde and of spiritually inferior people.

And all this with *the same* coloured stones!

It is exactly the same with man. Out of the same qualities, abilities and talents emerge the most varied individuals. But whether the result is an ignorant, undisciplined, inferior person, or, at the other end of the scale, a sublime, superior creature of possibly very high intelligence, depends upon the pattern which forms the basis of the person's make-up, that is to say, the way in which his qualities are related to one another.

While the artist, however, *consciously* creates a variety of pictures from his stones, man is completely *unaware* of the inner pattern or image which has formed his nature. In the case of a picture it is obvious how the stones are interrelated and therefore we clearly see what the picture represents, where it belongs, where it will ultimately be and what type of person it will please or displease. By the same token the whole 'destiny' of the picture can easily be foreseen. Man, however, can neither see his own image nor predict his fate. He does not see or know the pattern which is the basis of his character. Even less does he know that this inner pattern IS HIMSELF! If he knew this pattern which he is, if he had SELF-KNOWLEDGE, he could also clearly see before him his whole fate and advance along the path of life surely and confidently. The average person, however, knows neither himself nor his destiny and he gropes about in life like a child in the dark.

Yet already in prehistoric times there were, and there still are today, some initiates who knew and depicted in various pictures the 'coloured stones' which form the human image, that is to say, the spiritual elements and the abilities, qualities and talents developed therefrom, which in turn form the basis of a person's character according to his inner pattern. These pictures are so apt and created with such penetrating psychological insight that they depict not only the spiritual factor in question, but at the same time also its cause and effect. They do not, therefore, show only the fundamental qualities, abilities and characteristic features of man, but also their source and the responses they elicit in the world at large. In short, they show man's entire destiny.

These ancient prehistoric representations from which the complete picture of the most diverse kinds of people can be assembled and made accessible to our recognition are the tarot cards. This concept can be referred to as tarot.

The tarot comprises seventy-eight tarot cards. Of these, fifty-six cards are known as the Lesser Arcana and twenty-two cards as the Greater Arcana.

In order to understand the Lesser Arcana, we must remember that all the spiritual elements constituting a person spring from a single primal source in which everything still rests in unity. From this source all manifestations proceed step by step to the complete unfolding. We may compare this to the growth of a plant from a seed, through various stages of development, from the cotyledon, bud and flower, to its supreme achievement, the fruit. The initiates have depicted these stages in the growth of man in fourteen related pictures.

The first card carries the number ONE from which all further manifestations arise. From it derive the numbers up to TEN, which is again the number ONE, linked to the circle representing the universe, the cipher. These rising numbers show how man, from the beginning of his development, continues to grow in his abilities and in value until he detaches himself from the mob as an individual. Thus in the representations the ten numbered cards are followed by four court cards of ascending importance: the Page, Cavalier and Queen, and lastly the card dominating all others, the King. This shows the development of man from a weak personality to an ever-stronger one. Yet nonetheless, it is the first card, the number ONE, which has the highest value; in card games it is known as the Ace. The number ONE, the Ace, outranks all other cards for this is the only begetter of all the ensuing revelations. From it all other levels have proceeded. The ten numbered and the four court cards together make fourteen cards.

These fourteen levels of development manifest themselves through the four elements known in modern science as 'states of matter'. In the old terminology these are: fire, air (gaseous), water (liquid) and earth (solid). These elements are depicted on the cards by four different symbols: Rods, Swords, Coins and Cups. Under each of these symbols the fourteen levels of development are represented in fourteen cards; thus we arrive at four times fourteen, that is, fifty-six cards. These fifty-six cards are the 'Lesser Arcana' of the tarot deck.

The 'Greater Arcana' cards represent the principle which governs the qualities of man depicted by the fifty-six cards. This principle is the *consciousness* of man. For *how* and *to what purpose* he uses his abilities and talents, whether rightly or wrongly, to good ends or bad, depends upon the *level of his consciousness*. In order to preserve the analogy, we must remember that a mosaic is lifeless, consists of dead matter and is pieced together by an artist who *exists outside his work*. Man, however, is himself the artist who assembles his own personal image in accordance with the inner pattern, but from within, and it is he himself who reveals his inner image, his character, through his physical being. At the beginning of his development he is completely unaware of his position. He constructs his image unconsciously in accordance with natural laws. Since he lacks self-knowledge he lives within his own image like a prisoner in a cell which he has built himself, and instead of being its master he is its slave. Consequently he is also the slave of his own fate. While he is in this unconscious state, fate tosses him about like a rudderless ship in a tempest. In his despair man seeks and expects help from outside, never suspecting that real help, liberation from this blind groping, from this bondage, can be found in himself and himself alone.

Yet it is precisely through these strokes of fate brought upon himself in his ignorance that he awakes one day. He comes to his senses and grows conscious within himself. He notices that he is *here*, that he even exists! From this first awakening, however, from this initial flickering of self-awareness to the ultimate goal – divine and perfect universal consciousness – a long path of development lies before him. When he has reached this goal, and not before, man ceases to be encumbered with an unconscious at work under his consciousness. He has attained complete freedom. He has attained mastery over all the powers which have gone into his making and which work within him. What is more, the whole universe was formed by the same creative powers as man himself. Thus man is capable of controlling these powers in other people also and in the whole universe when he has made them conscious within him and learned to control them. In this state of consciousness he is master of all the abilities, qualities and talents which have formed his image in the world of matter. At the same time, however, he is master of his fate, for in this state he is no longer the unconscious pattern of his image, but has become the conscious creator of his own individuality and of his own world.

The initiates of prehistoric times who created the tarot cards were familiar with all these different levels and states of development of the human consciousness. They depicted these levels of consciousness from the first awakening to divine all-consciousness in twenty-two pictures. These are the 'Greater Arcana' of the tarot pack.

However far we may peer back into the dark recesses of history, it is impossible to find a period when these images, the Greater Arcana of the tarot cards, were not known. Already in ancient times we find traces of these cards; indeed they are the forerunners of all other playing cards. In the Babylonian, Egyptian, Judaic, Mexican, Indian and Chinese excavations, as well as those of even older cultures, evidence was found of the existence of these cards. Sometimes they were found as murals, sometimes as sculptures hewn in stone or as terracotta tablets. These finds are always and unmistakably representations of the tarot cards. Wherever they have been discovered, their resemblance is so striking as to point inevitably to a common provenance. What this original source is, however, we do not know.

Yet these finds are usually no more than fragments of the whole sequence. We should not possess complete packs of tarot cards had it not been for one nation which esteemed its religious traditions and holy scriptures so highly that it has preserved these unaltered over thousands of years to the present day. I am referring to the Jews.

The Jews received their sacred texts from Moses, who had been initiated in Egypt. He passed on to his people the deepest mysteries of the whole Creation and of human nature, the entire secret knowledge which he had learned from the Egyptian high priests in the temple. The Jewish high priests, the great initiated Rabbis, have preserved the Books of Moses unaltered to the present day. Not a single letter is ever allowed to be changed. The reason for this is very important: Moses wrote his books in Egyptian-Hebrew writing without vowels. Depending on which vowels we now insert between the consonants the text takes on a different meaning. For this reason it is most important that no letter be changed. Moses supplied his writings with a secret key that indicates how the vowels are to be inserted in the text. We find this key in the Cabbala.

The various parts of the Books of Moses together form the Tora.

The secret texts which also contain the key to the vowel insertion are: SEFER YETSIRAH (the Book of Creation), ZOHAR (light), to which belong also the TAROT and the CLAVICULA SALAMONIS (the key, the seal of Solomon). Together these form the Cabbala. Thus we see that the tarot is an important part of the Jewish scriptures. Cabbala means oral tradition.

The Cabbala is the science of GOD, of the nature of man, and of all the relations which exist between these. It teaches and proves that ALL IS IN ONE and ONE IN ALL! For before the divine will expels from itself the creative principle, the Logos, the UNIVERSE rests in the divine ONE, in GOD. When creation begins, all further numbers *ad infinitum* are born out of the number ONE. Yet the numbers are inseparably linked to the letters. For the first manifestation of the Logos, the first, very highest divine frequency which streaks through infinite space like the Horus bird setting Creation in motion, is the TONE, the SOUND, thus the letters. These first manifestations of the creative will, the vibrations of the TONE, form the entire Creation according to mathematical laws, divine ideas and thoughts. They act as an animating energy in every creature, be that a universe, sun, planet, crystallising stone, plant, animal or man. The great initiates knew the basic elements of the Creation and the link between the creative vibrations of the letters and numbers which act as mathematical laws in the Creation and realise creative ideas at the level of matter. From these basic elements and their relations they created pictures each representing a creative idea, thus a *concept*, a *letter* and a *number*. These pictures are the Greater Arcana of the tarot deck. Together they form the twenty-two letters of the primitive Hebrew alphabet.

Hebrew script, like all divine scripts, is written and read from right to left. Everything that is experienced in a divine state of being is exactly the reverse of that experienced, seen, that is to say, written or read, in a state of being which has fallen away from the divine state. For instance: the letter E as it stands here on the page is seen by everyone as facing from left to right. If, however, I *am* the E in a state of being, it is the other way round. Let us imagine that the E is drawn on our own chest, in which case everyone else will see it facing from left to right. I myself, however, will experience it from within towards the outside, from right to left, since *I am the E.* To experience the E is to *be* the E. Once we have understood that it will be clear to us why these divine scripts must all be written and read from right to left.

The meaning of the word tarot becomes clear when it is written in the shape of a circle so that one T is superfluous

T

O   A

R

If we read in an anti-clockwise direction we obtain the word TORA, which in Hebrew means LAW. If we read from below, again in the Hebrew manner, clockwise, we obtain the word ROTA, which alludes to the eternal rotation of the universe. Since each letter in the Hebrew alphabet is also a number, we simultaneously obtain a row of numbers when we form a word. If we add these up the result is a total sum of the digits. Therefore every word, every name, has a total sum. The Bible is written in such a way that the total sum of each word and name is much more significant than we at first suspect. Just one example: each time the name of the Messiah and that of his opponent, Satan, occur, the total sums of these two names are always the exact reflections of each other! And this rule, this interrelation between numbers and letters, prevails throughout the entire Bible. We can only wonder at the awe-inspiring knowledge with which the Bible was written!

In Europe there was another race besides the Jews who spread the fame of tarot: the Gypsies, who still use the tarot cards today for the purpose of foretelling the future. Although the pictures on their cards are to a great extent degenerate, in particular those of the Greater Arcana cards, they are immediately recognisable as tarot cards. With their primitive pictures they are known as 'Gypsy cards'. That the Gypsies received these cards from the Jews is very doubtful. The Jews jealously guard their secrets, their religious traditions, from the inquisitive eyes of the stranger, and it is not likely that they handed over these cards which form part of their sacred scriptures to the Gypsies. It seems much more probable that the Gypsies took over the tarot from the Egyptians or even older races.*

If what we have said has been correctly understood, it is clear that the tarot cards can be used like mosaic stones as it were, to represent man's exact spiritual image as well as his fate.

Yet how can the ignorant man spread out the exact picture of his soul like a mosaic if he does not know the inner pattern which controlled his own creation? Which pattern should he

---

* The English word 'Gypsy' seems to indicate that the Gypsies are taken to be Egyptians. Research has, however, shown that the Gypsies are of Indian origin. The Gypsy language and the names of the numbers are identical with those of the Hindus. But is it not true that both races, the Ancient Egyptians and the Indians, originate from the same native country, from Atlantis? There is much evidence to support this, particularly the remarks of Pythagoras on the subject.

choose when spreading out the mosaic stones, the tarot cards, in order to obtain a true picture?

There is a simple way of doing this and it can even be proven mathematically accurate by the theory of probabilities. No living creature, and therefore no man, can manifest anything other than what he himself is! His every remark, thought, word and deed reveal only what he himself is. His handwriting, his gait, the smallest of his gestures are the result of the forces at work in him. Nothing is chance, everything is the direct manifestation of the conscious or the unconscious Self. Hence, it is not mere chance *how* a person picks up the tarot cards, *how* he shuffles them, *how many* cards he lifts when cutting and *in what sequence* he consequently spreads the cards. Men discovered these facts already in ancient times or they learned them from initiates! That is why the art of spreading cards for the purpose of exploring a man's inner image and his future prospects is as old as mankind.

Thus we assume that in picking up the cards, shuffling, cutting and spreading them, we use the best method based on the experience of thousands of years, and that therefore we have spread out the image of our Self and of our destiny. Indeed, we have spread out our spiritual image before us, but we do not understand it! Understanding is only possible when we know the inner symbolic meaning of every single card, when we have penetrated it completely and grasped how the cards are related as they lie next to and on top of each other on the table, i.e. the effect which they exercise upon each other.

In order to understand our own image, it is therefore of the greatest importance that we know the meaning and inner sense of the individual cards. For the time being we merely look at the cards like an illiterate man at letters. For him letters are no more than black shapes on paper. That these are letters, how they are pronounced and what they are called, is a complete mystery to him. He understands neither the letters nor the words made from them, and still less the sentences constructed.

from the words. He does not suspect that these black shapes with the strange forms could mean something. In exactly the same way the uninitiated looks at the tarot cards. He understands neither the individual cards nor the meaning of their sequence. He does not even understand the letters and the numbers of the pictures, however well he can read and count. For on the tarot cards, these letters and numbers have a much deeper mystical meaning in the cabbalistic sense than ordinary letters and numbers. On these cards nothing is accidental, there is no line or colour without significance; they belong to the intrinsic meaning of the cards.

Yet for the person who understands them, these cards are a wonderful means of acquiring *self-knowledge*. For let us only think of this: when an ignorant man regards himself in the mirror he sees his reflection just as he has seen the cards spread before him. But just as he fails to understand the cards – he only *looks at them* – so also does he fail to understand his own reflected image. He only looks *at*, but not *into*, his image. Yet each line, shape and colour on his face and body has a deep inner significance. His outward image also conceals within itself the image of his invisible inner being, conscious as well as unconscious. Man has no idea that behind his outward image there is a very large part of his being hidden away in his unconscious, and that it is the great goal of our earthly existence to make this same unconscious attain consciousness within us. In this great task of awakening the unconscious and raising it to consciousness, thereby attaining perfect self-knowledge, the tarot cards are of unique assistance. The nature of these cards is such that they can produce a strong awakening effect on man's unconscious. He need only examine them one by one and, in order to understand them better, read the relevant description. When he reaches the card corresponding to his inner state, his interest will suddenly be roused and the knowledge that he finds himself at the level of consciousness of that particular card will hit him like an electric shock. This card he will understand completely, find full of life and meaning, and in the depths of his being he will feel a strong response. With the remaining cards he experiences the opposite. He will find these lifeless, uninteresting and dead, they convey nothing to him, and even if he comprehends them *intellectually* there is no echo in his soul. If he studies the cards one by one, a bright light will illuminate his soul by which he will see where he still has to work on himself and how he must change himself in order to achieve contentment.

That these cards help us to awaken our unconscious to consciousness so that we acquire self-knowledge – a thorough understanding of ourselves – can be testified by anyone who has picked them up and examined them one by one. They are like a spiritual mirror in which we can not only recognise but also thoroughly examine and study ourselves. We realise that in a strange way certain cards correspond exactly to our inner state, and at the same time also to our state in relation to the world. We suddenly understand ourselves and our destiny. We understand why fate always leads us back into the same predicament and why we have to solve the same problems again and again. We understand that the reasons for our fate *lie within ourselves.* Therefore we must *change ourselves* in order that our fate may also *change.* And our fate changes by the mere fact that we will begin to *react differently* to everything that happens to us.

These cards enable us to see clearly and to understand not only our present state but also our past and in a certain sense we will also be able to predict our future. Fate is the sum of the reactions to our actions. If we know which cards are representative of our inner state, then we will also be able to deduce from the cards what it was that made us act in a particular way. We will know too why we must bear the consequences of our deeds as 'fate'. And if we are not perfectly content and satisfied with our lives – and only rarely can we say that of ourselves – the cards will also enable us to discover *what* can help us out of our present situation and difficulties. Of course the inner states are an inherent part of us even when we do not pick up the cards. But they enable us to gain clear insight into our life and to solve our problems more easily and speedily.

Thus the spiritual powers of these strange cards begin to take effect in man and this effect is enhanced in proportion to his improved understanding of the cards. The stronger their effect on him, the greater his awareness of his Self and the more he will understand that these cards symbolise the fabric of his soul. Thus the tarot brings man ever closer to his great goal, which is to know himself, *to be himself.*

Some of the French titles on the twenty-two cards are misleading, but for technical reasons they could not be changed. The correct titles appear in the chapter headings.

THE MAGICIAN

Number: 1

Letter: א ALEPH

In this picture we see a strong young man, a magician, whose posture assumes the shape of the letter ALEPH. He leans slightly towards the right, pointing downwards with his right hand and upwards with his left. At the same time, this posture suggests the ancient truth which the great Chaldean initiate Hermes Trismegistos teaches in his TABULA SMARAGDINA HERMETIS: '*As above, so below.*'

The young man is dressed in garb of a curious colour. He is wearing a hat which, on careful examination, turns out not to be a hat at all. The crown of the supposed hat is the man's own head, a closed red circle symbolising his eternal spirit, his higher Self. Part of the circle is covered by the brim of the hat so that we do not see all of his head. This denotes that he is not yet fully conscious in his spirit, that there is still a great deal in his unconscious, in the invisible part of himself. The colour red indicates that the spirit, positive-giving, is a divine fire. It is in a closed circle because it can never show itself in the external world of matter. The spirit belongs to another world. In the world of matter it is invisible and cannot be perceived by any sense-organ. That is why it requires an instrument of manifestation through which it can reveal itself directly as idea, thought or knowledge. This instrument is the intellect, symbolised by the brim of the hat. This brim has the shape of the sign used by mathematicians to denote 'infinity', an 8 in a horizontal position: ∞. The edge of the brim is yellow, the colour of reason, and the inside of the brim is green, the symbol of sympathy, goodwill and amity. The young magician thus manifests his invisible, fiery, eternal spirit – which has never been born and therefore will never die – through the boundless infinity of thought and knowledge, but also through sympathy, goodwill and amity.

On his torso we see a red, tight-fitting tunic with a blue collar and a blue stripe down the front. The tunic is tight for the simple reason that it is not a tunic at all, but his own body. Red symbolises his spiritual being, which, like his head, is positive-giving. The blue of the collar and centre stripe edged in white symbolises his pure, selfless love of mankind. He bears this selfless love within, but also allows himself to be led by this universal love of mankind on his path through this world. This is shown by his legs which bear him along his earthly path and are clad in blue stockings.

His arms symbolise the two great polar principles of creation, the active-masculine, positive-giving pole, and the passive-feminine, negative-receiving pole. His arms are clothed in several coloured layers. This means that the magician uses his arms and hands in many different ways: with reason, as symbolised by yellow, and with good intentions and goodwill towards his fellow-men, as indicated by green, while under these two layers he wears a blue, tight-fitting, knitted garment, which, like the blue stripe on his torso, shows his own true being. The red cuffs denote that he continues to radiate spiritual, giving power, even if he lets himself be guided in his activity and work by his selfless love of mankind and by his humanity.

On the blue centre panel of his tunic we see five buttons. These are his five sense-organs through which he links himself, his inner world, with the external world!

Only three legs of the table in front of him are visible, the fourth juts out into the invisible spiritual world. The magician's activity rests for the most part on a material basis. His person lives in the visible world of matter, and so it is here that he must fulfil his task. Yet part of his actions, the fourth leg of the table, rests on invisible, spiritual foundations.

On the table lie three symbols of tarot, as yet unused but ready for use: the cup, the sword and the coin. He holds the most important symbol, the wand or baton, in his left hand. At each end of the wand is a coloured ball. These again symbolise the two polar principles, the red ball standing for the positive pole, the blue one for the negative pole. The magician holds the wand so that the positive end points upwards and the negative end downwards towards the coin. The wand symbolises the letter JAY, which is the picture of the first divine manifestation, a single flame, from which proceed all subsequent letters and gradually the whole of creation. In the magician's hand the baton becomes a magic wand. This is the creative power of the magician with which he realises the will of his higher Self in the visible world. With it he can effect true miracles and thus he gradually turns into a white magician.

The outside of the cup is blue, thus feminine-negative, receptive, but it contains the spirit, the masculine-positive, fiery principle represented by the red liquid inside the cup. The latter stands on a hexagonal base. It is formed by the two interwoven triangles which stand for the spiritual and the material worlds. The cup points to the magician's spiritual principles and signifies his receptivity to all that is good, to the divine higher truths of the spirit.

The sword also lies open, as yet unused, on the table. It symbolises the magician's courage with which – like Siegfried and the 'Nothung' against the dragon – he is prepared to fight against the shadows of the underworld, against the unconscious, in order to attain the divine light of consciousness.

Lastly, there is a gold coin lying on the table. The circular shape always stands for the spirit; but the cross drawn on the coin shows that in this case it is a very powerful and special spirit, which with its vast concentrating power creates *matter* and controls it thus unifying the two opposing elements. That is the coin, *money*. For the content of this concept 'money' is purely symbolical. How could anyone think of '*money*' as matter? Has anyone ever seen 'money' or held it in his hand? No one! At most we have seen or held a piece of paper or metal marked with a certain value. Therefore both are valuable only when they bear an inscription specifying that they represent a certain monetary value in which we have *to believe*. If, however, on the same note or coin there are no inscriptions denoting the particular value, then it is no longer 'money'. The moment we cease to believe in it, the note will become a worthless piece of paper and the coin will have no more value than the metal it is made of. But this, too, fluctuates according to demand. Remember that for a man dying of thirst in the desert any piece of metal, whether gold or silver, is utterly worthless. On the other hand, a glass of water would save his life. 'Money' is therefore a purely abstract notion rather than visible or tangible matter. It is the spirit of *absolute matter*, precisely because as a concept it cannot be identified with any kind of matter. And yet, we can acquire all the material treasures of the world with this nameless matter: real estate, jewels, furniture, clothes or whatever. Money is therefore the spirit of absolute nameless matter.

Nor does the coin in this picture of the magician suggest visible 'money' with an exchange value. It suggests much more, namely, man's inner spiritual power which allows him to control all the values of the material world, if he knows this secret! Our magician knows it for, of course, he already has power over the secret of 'money'.

Between his legs, just behind him, we see a flower which has grown out of the earth, and hence out of matter. It has three green leaves and a bud. The green leaves stand for the three great principles of spirit, power and matter. The closed flower, the bud, is red and thus denotes the spirit. This symbolises that the magician's spirit, like the bud, does not yet manifest itself completely. Like the flower, his spirit is already present, but in many respects still unconscious. Just as the flower does not yet unfold its inner splendour, so the magician also does not yet show the perfection of his spirit, of his higher Self. His very highest, divine treasures are still latent in his unconscious. That is also the reason why the flower is *behind* him, just as his unconscious is *behind* his consciousness. It is, however, only a question of time until the flower opens to reveal its glory and the magician manifests his innermost perfect being.

This picture, THE MAGICIAN, shows a man who has just awakened, suddenly become conscious in himself and perceives for the first time that he actually is *here* – that he is *here now*. Thus he experiences for the first time the absolute present in the state of self-awareness. His Self is boundless and infinite in the unconscious, just as his hat shows infinity, but the first flickering of self-awareness is still limited and its light is only the first divine spark not yet illuminating his whole divine being. He is still the divine child but is already the beginning, just as the child is the beginning out of which he grows to adulthood. In the same way, the number ONE is first in the sequence of numbers and the letter *aleph* is the beginning of the alphabet.

'The magician' represents a male or female being. That the state of awakening is depicted in this case as a man does not mean that only a man could experience this state. In the first state of self-awareness there is no sex. The human being, male or female, experiences a positive spiritual state; this state is represented by the picture of a man. A living creature at this level of consciousness is already in possession of all the divine gifts which continue to help him along the great path to self-knowledge.

The magician holds the 'magic wand' which he can use to open all the closed doors in his unconscious. His soul is like a cup from which he can already sip the divine nectar of the spirit. The sword, too, is already at his disposal so that he can vanquish the shadows of the underworld, of the unconscious, and win the divine light of the Self, of all-consciousness. And finally, he already possesses the gold coin, the spiritual power over all that is matter. He already knows the inner, divine value of all things, so that he will never again lose his way in the forest of the false material values of this world.

Although he possesses all these treasures, he is not yet an active 'magician'. Indeed he possesses these divine gifts, but he does not yet make use of them. He does not know that he already has all the attributes at his finger-tips for becoming a genuine white magician in the garden of God. He stands there still motionless, but ready to set out on the long path to self-knowledge.

The picture of the magician carries the number 1 and the letter *aleph*. The number 1 is the divine number which exists even before other numbers are born out of it. It is the father of all other numbers, it is indivisible and eternal. It is the only number which we can use as a multiplier without changing the value of the mutiplied number. The Vishnu-Purana says: 'There was neither day nor night, neither heaven nor earth, neither darkness nor light, nor any other thing, nothing but the ONE.' And Ramakrishna, the great Indian illuminate, states similarly: 'Know the One and you will know all.' The ciphers become hundreds of thousands if we place them behind the one. If, however, the one is extinguished, nothing remains. The many is only of value in relation to the One. First the One and then the many. First God and then the world and the creatures.

This card with the letter *aleph* corresponds to the first name of God as He named himself when Moses asked: 'If I come to the people of Israel . . . and they ask me, "What is his name?" what shall I say to them?'

God said to Moses, 'I AM WHO I AM.' (Exodus 2: 13–14)

In the Cabbala this card corresponds to the first choirs of angels which are called *Seraphim*. Until the time of the prophet Isaiah SERAPH signified a sacred serpent with three pairs of wings. Isaiah then took over this name for the angels. Since that time *Seraph* has been the name of an angelic being with three pairs of wings. SEFIROTH is a whole host of such angels. In the Cabbala there are ten such creative *sefiroth*. *Sefirah* literally means EMANATION (radiation). In modern scientific terminology the *sefiroth* would be known as 'emanating energy fields'. Each *sefirah* is both a number and a letter and has its corresponding attribute. That of the first *sefirah* is *Kether Elyon*, the 'supreme crown' which stands for the self-awareness of man. Just as a person is ruler of his country by virtue of a crown on his head, so consciousness of the Self gives him the power to become ruler over all the powers of the UNIVERSE. His self-awareness is the crown of his being.

In the Hebrew alphabet three letters are called 'mothers'. These three mothers are: ALEPH, MEM and SHIN. All three mean a birth and for that reason are known as 'mother'. *Aleph* is the first birth, the birth of the divine child, of SELF-AWARENESS. Man's purified soul gave birth to the divine child, the first flickering of self-awareness. Man is still like a child, only beginning to look about himself and not yet able to use his divine attributes, his God-given talents. In the course of time his activity will develop and only then will he become an adult. The letter *aleph* has thus given birth to the first awakening of consciousness in man.

The number 1 and the letter ALEPH are both the *beginning of a development*. Just as the divine number 1 gives rise to all subsequent numbers *ad infinitum*, so the letter ALEPH marks the beginning of the alphabet. Just as the bud is the beginning which leads to the full blossom, so the present consciousness of man with the magic instruments at its disposal is the beginning of the great, long and uneven path to the supreme goal, to perfect, divine ALL-CONSCIOUSNESS.

Tarot Card 2

THE HIGH PRIESTESS

Number: 2

Letter: ב Beth

In this picture we see a female figure clad in a priestly robe and seated on a strange throne, immobile, calm, inscrutable, mysterious and majestic. She is the high priestess of the temple and guardian of its secrets. She wears a tiara ringed by two gold bands, with a crescent moon on top. This crescent moon signifies that this figure represents a passive, female-receptive state in which man directs his whole interest and receptivity simultaneously to two planes: to this world and the other. These two planes, these two worlds, are also symbolised by the two gold bands on the tiara.

The face of the high priestess is partly covered with a white veil. This shows that she reveals by no means all of her nature. She wears a long, tight-fitting, blue dress. Blue denotes that in her innermost being she is filled with pure faith in God, selflessness and love of mankind. Over this dress she wears a red robe edged with yellow. Red shows the spirituality which she outwardly manifests in the world of matter. In so doing, she hides from inquisitive eyes her loving, innermost being symbolised by the colour blue. The yellow border signifies her reason, which she manifests through language and writing. The robe is fastened to her body by two broad straps on which there are several small crosses. These again signify the priestess's close relations both to the realm of the spirit and the realm of matter.

In her right hand she holds a half-closed book which contains, but as yet does not yield, the mysteries of this world and the other. On the cover of the book is the Chinese symbol of the deity resting in itself, Yang and Yin, in which the two poles still rest in one unity in God. Only in their manifestations are these two worlds, the external material world, and beyond this the inner spiritual one, ostensibly separated from each other. In the inner reality they always belong together, they cannot possibly exist without each other. For it is on the tension existing between them in the world of matter that the whole of Creation is based.

In her left hand she holds two keys. These are the keys to this world and the next. She has access to both worlds, she can lock or unlock the gates, enter or leave as she pleases. But she does not divulge the mysteries of these worlds to the immature.

She is seated on a throne. On either side of the back of the throne are two tall pillars. Simply the colours above reveal that the right-hand pillar is fiery, masculine-spiritual, and the left-hand one moist, feminine-feral. These are the two pillars of King Solomon, Jachin and Boaz, on which he built his temple. They are also the two legs of Logos in Revelation. One foot stands on the land, the other on the sea. These two pillars sustain the tension between the two creative poles, the positive and negative one, on which, as the Bible says, the creative principle, Logos, rests as it creates the universe. There is a curtain between the pillars. It corresponds to the veil of the Egyptian goddess Isis. In the Hindu philosophy of religion this curtain is the veil of *maya*. It screens the mysterious absolute reality resting in man's unconscious, but which the immature man cannot and is not permitted to see. The secrets of the unconscious are still hidden from his eyes, but he already suspects the titanic powers at work below the level of his consciousness. He believes that the phenomena he perceives do not arise from his own unconscious but from outside. Thus he begins to concern himself with the phenomena of occultism. He attends spiritualist meetings where, as he believes, the 'spirits' of the departed manifest their presence and transmit messages from the hereafter. He also goes to other circles and societies which pursue all kinds of 'sciences of the occult'. Thus he becomes a 'seeker'.

The floor on which the high priestess sits is made up of two kinds of coloured tiles, black and white stone squares laid out like the squares of a chess-board. The white tiles symbolise the spiritual, invisible world, and the black tiles the material, visible world. Just as these various squares are combined on the floor, so, in the soul of the seeking man, the two worlds are *combined*, but not yet united. He already begins to grow spiritual, but is still essentially in the bondage of matter.

One arm-rest of the throne represents a black sphinx and the other a white one. Only the black sphinx is, however, visible; the white sphinx is still hidden from view under the high priestess's robe.

The sphinx is a very important stage on the path to self-knowledge. In Greek mythology we read that people asked Oedipus, loudly lamenting, to save them from the monster, the terrible sphinx, who sat on the clifftop looking down to the plain and poisoning the pure air with her breath. If help did not come at once all the people of Cadmus would perish and die. Every day she uttered her incomprehensible words and devoured each man who failed to solve her riddle. Oedipus asked what this riddle was. The wailing people replied: 'The sphinx says no more than this: "What is it that has one voice and yet becomes four-footed and two-footed and three-footed?"' And Oedipus went to the sphinx and when she posed the same question he answered: 'Man, who crawls on all fours in infancy, walks on two feet when grown and leans on a staff in old age.' And with a terrible roar the sphinx leaped down from her cliff and ran away.

The riddle of the sphinx is thus the great riddle of man. And in this picture, as the arm-rest of the throne, this sphinx is also the great riddle of man – self-knowledge.

The high priestess's left arm rests on the visible black sphinx, and her right arm on the *as yet* invisible white sphinx. The whole picture of the high priestess shows the state of the newly awakened human being, who, for the very first time, has experienced the stirrings of self-awareness. He has learned that an 'other world' exists besides this earthly material one. His interest turns to this 'other world' which is to be found beyond his consciousness. He begins to wonder about the hereafter and wanders from one so-called 'spiritual society' to another. He goes wherever he senses a possibility of solving the great riddle of BEING. He already suspects that he is not in this world for the sole purpose of fulfilling earthly duties. These duties are also 'his' duties, for the additional and very good reason that these and *only these* can help him to reach the great goal of his life, the attainment of self-knowledge. What this great goal is, he does not yet know, but he feels that this life still owes him something, that it must bring him something wonderful which he has waited for all his days. This must be fulfilment, redemption. He does not yet clearly recognise that this goal consists in nothing other than the sweeping aside of the veil of the *maya*, the veil of illusions, renouncing all errors, discovering his own true Self and raising it to full consciousness. He knows only the worldly, conscious side of his own being, his apparent Self which he *is not*, while his own spiritual being still rests in his unconscious. Since he does not even know where to start seeking it, he seeks the hereafter and what happens after death. He wishes to know where the departed go, because he knows that he too will go there. But the high priestess who guards all these secrets does not yet take the great key and unlock the gate to the hereafter for him. Nevertheless he feels that behind this curtain he will find the solution to the riddle, the whole truth. And so he pursues his search. He goes on to learn philosophy and psychology, studies the philosophies of religion of all countries, and pursues all the Arts. It is only a question of degree whether he becomes an earnest seeker or a charlatan. For behind the serious research of the scholar, as behind the various childish amusements of the charlatan, lies the same desperate search by man for the great divine mysteries of eternal BEING!

The picture of the high priestess carries the number 2 and the letter BETH. The number 2 embodies the idea of division. There is no unity in existence which could contain the number 2. If, however, this number nevertheless lodges itself in a unity, this signifies a schism, disintegration of the unity concerned, and, in the case of a human soul, death. This state is expressed by the number 2 in every language of the world.* In this picture the number 2 denotes the two worlds, here and beyond, which the seeking man bears within him and which bring about an inner conflict. This torments him and he seeks release, 'redemption' from it. On the one hand he still belongs here in the temporal world with its earthly joys and sorrows, on the other hand he is already interested in *what* lies behind it, *what purpose* it all serves if in the end we have to leave everything here, and *what* the values are that we can finally take with us. And if we succeed in taking something with us, *where* shall we go with it? This *whither* is what interests him, for he has already realised that this world is only the *effect*, but not the *cause*. This world is not an absolute reality, it is only a world of appearance. Yet where is the absolute reality, the eternal, immortal cause? He knows that where there is an effect there must also be a cause. And the cause of this world is what man seeks to find.

The high priestess, however, does not raise the curtain before the sacred shrine, but lets the immature man continue to seek the truth by himself. If she were to reveal the nature of this truth to man, he would not gain anything by it. On the other hand, if he himself seeks this truth, he will find it in

---

* The author here draws attention to the German word '*Verzweiflung*' containing the number two – *zwei*.

reality – HE WILL BE THIS TRUTH HIMSELF! – To understand through reason is all very well, but that which has been understood is still outside and not inside man. Reason is merely an instrument which helps us to understand. Yet this understanding is still very far from realisation. We do not seek words, but the meaning of words, the reality, which we can never experience through reason but can only *be ourselves*.

In hieroglyphic writing, the letter BETH symbolises the human mouth. The high priestess as yet keeps her lips closed. She betrays nothing of her secrets and yet implies that they exist, so that man does not merely stand there, but is lured into seeking them himself. He will find them!

The letter BETH designates the second host of angels. It is the second *sefirah* and corresponds to *Hokhmah, theoretical reason*.

THE QUEEN

Number: 3

Letter: ‫ג‬ GIMEL

Again we see a young woman, this time without a veil. Her beautiful face freely reveals her nature. She faces us, she looks into our eyes, she does not wish to hide anything from us.

She wears a triple-pointed crown on her head. This denotes that she is queen of the three aspects of life: birth, life and death. It also means that she reigns over space, over the three dimensions. She is ruler of the whole cosmos, the whole universe. She is the queen of heaven, that aspect of God which is procreative and feminine: NATURE.

She sits perfectly motionless on her throne, just as her laws also are inflexible and unchangeable. She bears in her nature the great secret, the mystery whereby the spirit unites with matter and the divine becomes the human. This is the mystery of *procreation.* She herself, however, is the great chaste virgin who brings forth myriads of living creatures without having been touched by man. The two worlds, this world and the other, which in the case of the high priestess were still separated, are united in the queen of heaven. She holds sway over the spiritual and the material worlds because she has the power to join them together or to keep them apart. It rests with her and her laws whether a spirit embodies itself in this world and is born, or whether such an embodied spirit frees itself from the material world and its body dies.

Her head is framed by a white circle symbolising the immaculate purity which she radiates. In the circle we see twelve stars, three of which are hidden behind her head. These twelve stars are the signs of the zodiac, the twelve spheres of heaven as it were, by which her dominion over the universe is symbolised.

She has a pair of large, light blue wings, which, when spread out, enable her to hover above infinite space and to fly.

Her tight-fitting dress is red, suggesting that in her innermost being she is completely spiritual, positive. The yellow edging shows her superior reason, which she manifests through the brains of men.

Across her lap and right arm is draped an azure blue robe covering her legs as it falls to the ground. The robe and its brilliant blue colour symbolise the infinite firmament which is her kingdom; they are also a symbol of her immaculate purity. The green inner side of the blue robe signifies her goodwill and sympathy to all living things, to all her children.

The magic wand of the magician has in her hand become a long sceptre crowned with the symbol of the earth, an imperial orb. This symbol consists of a ball surmounted by a cross. It signifies that here on earth the law of matter prevails and that the spirit must bow to this law. The sceptre shows the immense and overwhelming power of Nature over the three worlds: heaven, earth and hell. The laws of Nature are immutable. The queen holds the sceptre in her left hand thus indicating that she rules with the irresistible power of the eternal-feminine and of the mother. She holds a shield bearing the great symbol of the alchemists, the white eagle on a red background. The white eagle symbolises the purity and chastity of the queen of heaven, the transformed sexual energy which she herself uses in its spiritual form only, as creative power. The eagle turns his head to the left, which again suggests the negative-feminine power of the queen. The red background shows that this power is based on the positive powers of the spirit.

The queen's right foot is completely hidden. She rests her left foot on a crescent moon pointing *downwards*. A crescent moon in the reverse position, pointing upwards, denotes receptivity to the high *spiritual* powers. The downward position denotes receptivity to *masculine potency*. The queen of heaven does not allow herself to be fertilised by the material earthly procreative power, she is chaste and remains so, but she does allow the separated sexes to reunite in their material form in her realm, in Nature. She allows the feminine, the receiving, to be fertilised and gratified by the masculine, positive-giving. Thus she succeeds in changing the divine into the human, in uniting the spirit with matter, in uniting the spiritual and material worlds in a new living creature. The queen of heaven, Nature, makes possible the embodiment of the spirit in the world of matter.

Next to the queen a white lily blossoms on the throne. It is also a symbol of her purity and chastity, but especially of her *health*. Nature strives unremittingly to keep her children, myriads of living creatures, healthy, to instil into them the instinctive urge always to do what is best for their health. And if in spite of this they do become ill, she helps to restore their health. The lily has a very strong healing power: it is rightly the symbol of health and purity.

We find this beautiful figure of a divine woman in all great religions as the feminine aspect of God. She is Nature, the great mother who gives birth to myriads of living creatures and has command over life and death. Her name alone varies from one race to another. The Ancient Egyptians knew her as the heavenly goddess ISIS, in the Hindu religion she is the worshipped great mother KALI, and in the Christian religion she is the MADONNA. In the Revelation of St John she is described as follows: 'And there appeared a great wonder in heaven, a woman clothed with the sun, and the moon under her feet, and upon her head a crown of twelve stars.' (Rev.12:1)

The man who is at this level of the tarot becomes acquainted with the great queen of heaven, NATURE. He is a 'seeker' and now he begins to explore the secrets of Nature. He no longer tries to act against Nature by leading a foolish life, but rather now adapts himself to her in order to live *with* and not against her. He experiences the inner command: GOOD HEALTH IS A DUTY! He tries to let the powers of Nature work in his body to make it healthy and preserve it in that state. He begins to experiment with various cures and diets, he eliminates meat from his diet as well as artificially produced drinks which rouse and stimulate his low impulses. Thus he grows familiar with the inner desires of Nature which were always latent in him as animal instincts but to which he had never paid heed. Thus he becomes reconciled with Nature, against whom he has so often sinned. He recognizes her as the dominating force in the visible world and in his body. As a result of these endeavours, however, he observes that each physical pheno-menon has an emotional cause, that each illness can therefore be traced to an emotional disturbance.

Thus we discover that if we look after our souls, achieve an inner harmony and spiritual health, our bodies also will become healthy. This truth leads us to the fresh discovery that there exists something beyond the dominion of Nature. What is more, this something can rule over Nature. This is our own spirit, our own higher Self. We discover that we are able to make ourselves master of Nature, to control and work with the forces of Nature, if our Self has become master in our soul and in our body. But only if first of all we recognise the laws of Nature! For if we do this, then we shall be able to let these titanic forces work for us not only in ourselves but also in the external world. The miller can only have his corn ground by the current of the water because he recognises the laws of Nature, of water, and builds his mill with the mill-wheel so placed that it is turned by the stream and grinds his corn.

Thus the 'seeker' tries to recognise the laws of Nature, but nevertheless to let them act within him in accordance with his own will. He removes all the obstacles which his foolish way of life had placed in the path of Nature. He begins to practise self-control and mental concentration.

In this way he unites in himself the two worlds, this one and the other, which, while still at the level of the 'high priestess', he wanted to know separately. He lets his spirit, his Self, which always has been and will be in the non-material, other world, rule in his physical being; he ceases to be a slave of his physical desires and tries to use his body as a wonderful instrument. Yet he does not on this account neglect his body; indeed, he gives it careful attention, for otherwise it could not manifest his spirit completely and perfectly. He does not forget that his Self has also helped to assemble his body. He realises that his body is his image, that his body is himself, even if only the most distant manifestation of his own spirit. He takes a big step forward, for he perceives that there is only *one* all-embracing, boundless universe, that the whole Creation is a single, indivisible unity.

The picture of the queen carries the number 3 and the letter GIMEL. The number 3 stands for absolute harmony and balance. The three corners of the equilateral triangle are equidistant from one another so that their connection does not result in insoluble tensions, as is for instance the case with the square and all other geometric figures. The number 3 also signifies the Holy Trinity and the three aspects of God, the creative, the preserving and the destroying aspect. All creative factors have three aspects. They are the three dimensions of space: length, breadth and height; the three aspects of time: past, present and future; the three aspects of earthly life: birth, life and death; and the three worlds under the rule of the queen of heaven: heaven, earth and hell. All these aspects are the three manifestations of a single unity. At the level of the 'queen of heaven' man consciously unites all these aspects in one being, in himself. He lives in the three dimensions, in space, he lives in time, he is aware that his body was born and that it will die, therefore he manifests all three aspects of life, even while realising that all these aspects concern only his mortal being. His true Self, his divine being, does not know all these aspects. It knows neither time nor space, birth nor death, past nor future, it knows only eternity and eternal life. It knows only the absolute present, 'the eternal Now'. And man now understands also that heaven, earth and hell are three states of consciousness, and that according to whichever level he identifies himself with, he is happy or unhappy. If he identifies with himself, with his spirit, and seeks spiritual joys, he is happy, therefore in heaven. During his life on earth he has experienced joys and sorrows, but these are both transient. And if he identifies with his impulses and becomes a slave of his body, he loses himself, despairs and in so doing plunges into hell.

At this level of consciousness man has understood Nature, the queen, and tries to put the truths which he understands well in theory, into practice, into realization.

The letter GIMEL means the human throat, where all the words born in the brain are formed. This letter is the symbol of the material manifestation of intellectual ideas. In the Cabbala it is the third *sefirah* and corresponds to *Binah*, practical reason.

Tarot Card 4

THE KING

Number: 4

Letter: ד DALETH

This is the picture of a strong man with all the attributes of a ruler. He is seated upon a cube as upon a throne. He is ruler of the world of matter. The Romans called him Jupiter. His seated position on the cube also represents the sign of Jupiter: ♃. The line curving upwards rests on the symbolic sign of matter, the cross.

The king wears a yellow helmet adorned with red and shaped into six points at the top like a crown. These points allude to the six-pointed star, formed by two interwoven triangles. When these are projected into the third dimension, two interwoven tetrahedrons are formed, which are concealed inside the cube.

The yellow colour of the helmet shows that the king manifests his high spiritual powers and wisdom in thought, speech and writing. The red contours of his helmet again point to his spirituality and wisdom. The dark colour of his hair and beard is a symbol of his concern with the material world. In Roman mythology he is Jupiter, in Greek mythology, Zeus, the god of wisdom and the heavenly ruler of earth.

The garment next to his body is red, again symbolising the spirituality of his innermost being. It is visible only on his

legs, knees and arms. The remaining part of it is covered by
other articles of clothing. On his chest and shoulders he wears
a light blue coat of mail. On the right side we see the sun, on
the left, the moon. The coat of mail shows his imperviousness
and power of resistance against foes and external attacks. The
sun and moon show that he unites in himself the two great
energies, the positive-masculine energy of the sun and the
negative-feminine energy of the moon, that he controls both
of them and works with them in the universe. Round his neck
he wears a thick golden chain, a symbol of his strong reason.

The coat of mail is decorated with a red fringe in a geometric pattern trimmed with yellow and partly covering his
blue uniform and blue sleeves. He therefore manifests spirituality, goodwill and kindness. His feet are clad in blue stockings; this means that his steps are always guided by pure love
and humanity. In his right hand he holds a mighty sceptre
which ends in three large leaves forming a *fleur de lys*. By
holding the sceptre in his right hand the king shows that he
works with positive-masculine forces.

In his left hand he holds a green imperial orb. This signifies
that he has power over the earthly world. This power, however, is not sheer force, but the irresistible power of universal
love. That is why the imperial orb is so large and green.

The king is seated upon a large yellow cube bearing the
picture of a brown eagle. The cube is the simplest crystallisa-
tion form of matter, the crystal form of salt.* That the king
sits upon a cube suggests that although he stands above matter
with his spirituality, he nevertheless needs matter and the
material world as a stable basis for his activity. He controls
matter and in addition uses it to gain spiritual powers from
material forces by transformation. In order to show this he
places his legs so as to form a cross, the symbol of matter.

The cube signifies a very fine type of matter through which
he manifests his wisdom. This matter is the human brain. That
is why the cube is yellow in colour. It is intelligent matter.

* cf. E. Haich, *Initiation*.

Through their brains men manifest the higher truths and the divine ideas of the king of heaven. Without this the king could not express and pass on his wisdom in thought, speech and writing. The dark eagle is the symbol of matter, but he no longer crawls on the ground as a scorpion manifesting base instincts but now serves the intellectual world by manifesting superior thoughts and soars in the air as an eagle. He turns his head to the right thus indicating that the power which the king uses is always of a masculine-positive, giving nature. We shall understand the significance of this cube even better if we think of the Ka'ba, which is the focal point of the religious cult of Islam in Mecca. The Ka'ba is a cube-shaped edifice, and according to tradition, was built in its present form by Abraham himself. Muslims throughout the world orient themselves towards it in prayer. And every Muslim who can makes a pilgrimage once in his life to the Ka'ba. Inside the Ka'aba there are twelve silver lamps suspended between three pillars with a thirteenth lamp in the centre. The three pillars symbolise the Holy Trinity and the twelve lamps stand for the twelve signs of the zodiac round the sun. There are no windows in the Ka'ba and only one door, which is seven feet above the ground and and can be reached by climbing a seven-runged ladder. The Muslims call the Ka'ba 'The House of God', which simply means man himself. As the symbolism of the Ka'ba is so clear we hardly need to explain that it is the cube, matter, the human body, the dwelling-place of the divine Self, of GOD. The three pillars represent the Holy Trinity which animates the body with the divine powers of Logos. Christ said '. . . for, behold, the kingdom of God is within you'. (Luke, 17: 21) The same symbol, the cube containing the divine principle depicted here as the Lamb offering itself in sacrifice, occurs in Revelation. John recounts his vision:

'And there came unto me one of the seven angels . . . and talked with me, saying, Come hither, I will shew thee the bride, the

Lamb's wife. [Man's consciousness which seeks unity with the divine principle] . . .

And he carried me away in the spirit to a great and high mountain, and shewed me that great city, the holy Jerusalem descending out of heaven from God . . .

And he that talked with me had a golden reed to measure the city, and the gates thereof, and the wall thereof . . .

And the city lieth foursquare . . . *The length and the breadth and the height of it are equal.* [Therefore it is cube shaped!] . . .

. . . and the city was pure gold . . .

. . . and the street of the city was pure gold, as it were transparent glass . . .

And I saw no temple therein: for the Lord God Almighty and the Lamb are the temple of it.

And the city had no need of the sun, neither of the moon, to shine in it: for the glory of God did lighten it, and the Lamb is the light thereof.' (Revelation 21 : 9–23)

As we can see, the visionary of the Bible also perceived the body of the illumined and redeemed man as a cube which had become transparent, the crystallised prototype of matter from which shines the light of God, the divine principle offering itself in sacrifice, the Lamb with its celestial light.

In front of the king we see the same flower that we saw behind the magician as a bud. There, the flower implies that man has not yet grown conscious and that the greatest part of his being still lies *behind* his consciousness, in his unconscious. Here, the flower is *in front of* the king of heaven and is already beginning to open. It is no longer a bud. At this level man is already considerably more aware than at the level of the 'magician'. He has power over his own body, over his material form. To a certain extent he already possesses self-control. He uses his body as a source of energy and transforms physical energies into spiritual powers, thereby quickening his progress on the long path to the great goal. His soul is now no longer a bud; it gradually unfolds and radiates the divine light, love. It dawns on him that our spiritual level does not depend upon how much we know, but upon how much love we have in us. What he has learned and grasped intellectually must be realized. He must not keep his experiences and knowledge for himself, he must pass them on to the uninitiated who come after him. He already has self-control and is master of physical desires. He uses the power thereby gained to help not only himself but also his fellow-men. He sees the great goal and devotes his whole life to the task of growing more spiritual, while leading others also to spirituality. He has read and learned a great deal and heard divine truths from great men who have reached the goal. At the same time, however, he has already gathered a store of individual experience and can thus pass on its treasures to others. More and more people come to him to ask for advice and help and he tries to alleviate human suffering. He gives help where possible and compassion and universal love unfold in his heart just as the flower opens its sepals.

The picture of the king carries the number 4 and the letter DALETH.

The number 4 as a geometric shape, as a square or cross, is found in the cube.

For if we open out a cube, we get a cross. All six sides of a cube are rectangular squares. Throughout the world and in every religion, the square and the cross are symbols of matter. On the two beams of the Cross, on time and space, the spirit of the world, Logos, Christ, is crucified. At the point of intersection of the two beams is the absolute present. Here time and space unite. For us, as embodied spirits, this point, the absolute present, is our only possibility of attaining REDEMPTION, LIBERATION while still in the body. Otherwise we are 'crucified' in time and space. If we manage to endure in the absolute present with absolute consciousness we are liberated from the 'crucifixion' in time and space. Then we are resurrected in eternity. The crucified human body is a symbol as old as mankind itself. Such crucifixes, thousands of years old, have been found in excavations all over the world, in America and in the Orient.

The number 4 also occurs as a symbol in the four great rivers which rise in the middle of Paradise and flow in the four directions of heaven. Equally so in the four great signs of the zodiac in Ezekiel's vision: lion, bull, angel and eagle; and likewise in the four faces of God in the Hindu philosophy of religion.

The tarot card KING complements the tarot card QUEEN. The king is the positive-masculine, and the queen the negative-feminine side of a single divine unity. The numbers 3 and 4 together make 7 which is the key number of the earthly world. That is why there are seven rungs on the ladder leading up to the Ka'ba in Mecca. If we add up the number 7 according to the principles of numerology, $1+2+3+4+5+6+7$, we get the number 28. The sum of the digits of the number 28 is the divine number of perfection, the fulfilment of creation, the number 10. The cipher has no numerological value because it symbolises space. Thus we are left with the divine number 1 as the final result. The result is the same if we add up the number 4 according to these principles, $1+2+3+4 = 10$. The final result is again 1.

The letter DALETH is the picture of the animating and active principle of the universe. Through it God depicts the images of the body and all the different forms of matter. DALETH corresponds to the fourth *sefirah, Hesed,* which means love and kindness.

THE HIGH PRIEST

Revealer of Sacred Things

Number: 5

Letter: ה HE

In this picture we see a male figure with all the insignia of an important dignitary of the church. He is the high priest. He sits upon a throne of which only two posts are visible. There is no longer a curtain between them, for there is nothing to hide any more. The face of the high priest, too, is without a veil. He shows us his face openly, he also has nothing to hide.

His white hair and beard show that he is a spiritual being which will itself never become earthly even though it is active in the earthly-material world. He always remains spiritual.

The high priest wears a yellow tiara with three golden circlets, ending at the top in the symbolic sign of the material world, a cross. The three circlets symbolise the three worlds over which the high priest has power: heaven, earth and hell. He can open or close these to man: he can lead him into or out of them.

His clothing is similar to that of the high priestess. His innermost being is imbued with universal love. For that reason he wears a blue robe on his body. Over it he wears a flowing red cloak covering his whole figure. Through this cloak he reveals his high spirituality. The yellow border indicates that he manifests his spirituality through thoughts and words. The green inner side of the cloak signifies sympathy, goodwill and friendliness.

He wears white gloves with blue crosses on the back. This means that even though he comes into contact with the world of matter, his hands always remain clean in spite of all the impurities of this earthly world. In his left hand he holds a sceptre which ends in a triple cross. Like the golden circlets on his tiara, it symbolises the three worlds: heaven, earth and hell.

Two figures kneel before him. Their clothing in itself reveals that they are two complementary opposites. One has a red collar and dark robe, the other a dark collar and a red robe. One has fair, the other dark hair. Together they symbolise the positive and the negative pole, but at the same time also the two sexes, the positive-masculine and the negative-feminine. They listen to the teaching of the high priest. The dark-haired male figure looks up at him and listens reverently. The fair female figure buries her face in her hands and appears to be afraid. The dark-haired man lays his hand encouragingly on her back. They symbolise the inner spiritual state of a man who is at the level of the tarot card 'high priest'. His positive-masculine nature already has the courage to follow his inner conviction, but the earthly-physical part of him is afraid and makes him feel that he might lose something of value. The truth, however, works strongly within him and through each new experience he grows more spiritual. This gives him power to live by his deepest conviction. He senses that we do not have to be *of* this world, even though we *live* in this world. He knows that he must come to terms with his impulses and bring them under control. He has made such progress in acquiring self-control that he has triumphed over the instinct of self-preservation. He no longer needs food and drink as stimulants. In other words, he has conquered his appetites. Now he still has to put his sex life in order and direct it into the right channels. He understands that he is not only a sexual being but, over and above his sexuality, a *human being*. He realises that his spirit is sexless, and that if a person awakes and grows conscious in his spirit, he will no longer think of himself as 'woman' or 'man', but as a 'human being'. He knows that when we reach our goal we become androgynous. Even though his body manifests only one half of the whole, thus *one* sex, his consciousness is above sexuality. He tries to live according to this insight and to become childlike, even if he does not always succeed.

During this period of work he learns many new truths. He learns from personal experience that his body is not merely an empty shell for his spirit, but that the powers of the spirit pervade the body in the same way as water can saturate every pore of a sponge. And the powers of the body, which flow from the spirit, but already act as physical forces on his consciousness, are just as strong as he is himself because, in the form of matter, these powers ARE HIMSELF. That is why it is so difficult to control these powers in oneself and to remain above them in one's consciousness: because we are confronting *ourselves*. His higher Self instructs him just as the high priest teaches the two figures. And he sees and understands ever more clearly the close relationships between his spiritual Self and his primitive drives which as yet refuse to release him. The truth, however, is stronger, and he realises that he is able to experience real joys and true, fulfilling love in physical union only if that union is the manifestation of a much deeper spiritual oneness. And he begins to seek in his partner, first and foremost, understanding and friendship, thus an inner relationship and a meeting of the minds. He realises that parallel to his inner life he must also create order and harmony in his outer life in order to solve his problems; and in order to achieve inner satisfaction he must not fail to bring the external and the inner world to a common denominator. Strange to say, fate helps him in this, for as if an invisible power witnessed his inner struggles, Providence brings him fresh possibilities and tasks in his earthly personal life. The mere fact that more and more people come to him to ask his advice and help forces him to abandon his previous way of life. He has got to organise his life in such a way that he can devote more time and energy to his fellow-men. In so doing he himself gets to know life from different angles and learns to occupy himself with the many difficult problems which those seeking help submit to him. And thus he perceives that heaven, earth and hell, do, in fact, exist, not as places but as human states. Just where his good or evil way of life will take him ultimately depends upon man himself. It gradually dawns on him that a suffering man suffers because he has become ready for a new, higher level. The suffering man has reached a new milestone on the great path. The suffering compels him to climb the next step at which his afflictions abruptly cease, because the problems which had hitherto seemed difficult and oppressive now show themselves to be less serious when seen from an entirely different angle.

Thus man struggles within himself as well as in the outer world. Through this struggle he makes progress, climbs higher, his horizon widens and he grows increasingly conscious in his being.

The fifth tarot card, the 'high priest', carries the number 5 and the letter HE.

Initiates call the number 5 the number of Christ or the number of Logos. The divine number of fulfilment, of creation, is the number 10. Half of this sum is 5. The symmetry in the bodies of living creatures implies that Logos divides the divine number 10 into two symmetrical sides, and in both parts half of the number 10 is at work, that is, the number 5. Human beings have 5 fingers on each hand, thus on both hands together 10 fingers. Likewise we have 5 toes on each of our two feet. We have 32 teeth, the sum of the digits is 5. The upper jaw has 16 teeth, total of the digits is 7, the lower jaw also has 16 teeth, total sum 7. Together these sums add up to 14, sum of the digits again 5. Thus the number of Christ appears again and again. The number of the senses is also 5 : sight, hearing, smell, taste and touch. And if we add up the limbs, two arms and two legs together with the head, we have the 5 extremities

of the human body, or again the number 5. The human body
fits into the five-pointed star and the vital current circulates
in the body in the shape of this star. That is why the right side
of the body is animated by positive current, and the left side
by negative current. Since the number 5 is itself half of the
number of perfect creation – the number 10 – it has an inner
relationship to the number 2 which is always retained. For
multiplying by the number 5 means *dividing* by 2 and multiplying the result by 10 (a very simple operation). Dividing a

sum by the number 5 means *multiplying* the number by 2 and
then dividing by 10. The numbers 5 and 2 are complementary
and together make the key number 7 which, by cabbalistic
reduction, leads again to the number 10 as the sum of the digits,
$1+2+3+4+5+6+7 = 28$, $2+8 = 10$. The fact that the
number 10 manifests itself in Nature as two complementary,
symmetrical halves – as twice 5 – as the five fingers on each
hand, etc., curiously emerges also when we add the numbers
from 1 to 10: $1+2+3+4+5+6+7+8+9+10 = 55$,
together, $5+5 = 10$! Tarot card 5, the 'high priest', complements tarot card 2, the 'high priestess', for the same reason.

In the Cabbala, the letter HE corresponds to the fifth
sefirah, which is called *Gevurah*, meaning fear, judgement and
strength. In hieroglyphics it means breath. Life is continuously
created and preserved by breath and from this arises the idea
of complete spiritualisation.

THE PARTING OF THE WAYS

Number: 6

Letter: ۱ VAU

In this picture we again see the 'magician'. This time he does not wear the hat representing his infinite spirit. Therefore what happens to him here does not concern his spirit. His fair hair falls loosely, its flaxen colour reveals his high intelligence. His tunic is red and green. The colours are reversed on the short skirt, green on his right and red on his left. The colours on his legs correspond to those on his chest. The sleeves are yellow. This clothing signifies that his whole being and his every step are guided by spirituality, charity and humanity. Inwardly, too, he is imbued with these principles. His activity, represented by his arms, is guided by his reason. He always considers carefully the rights and wrongs of what he is about to do. His hands are crossed on his breast as if he were shielding himself against an external influence. His eyes are downcast. He avoids suggestive glances which seek to penetrate him. Above his head is a twelve-pointed star and inside it a circle with an angel who, with drawn bow, is about to shoot an arrow at the magician. The twelve points of the star denote the twelve signs of the zodiac, and hence the creative energies which organise the visible world.

The young man stands at the parting of the ways with a female figure on either side of the fork. On his right we recognise the queen of heaven with the crown on her fair curled hair and her red and blue dress. On his left we see a woman with dark hair: she wears a yellow dress under a green cloak. We already know that yellow is the colour of reason, but in this case, yellow, the narrow red neckband, the red belt and the red flower in her hair are symbols only of her cunning and egoistic calculation which is devoid of true spirituality and belief. The colour blue is missing. The green cloak symbolises that she puts on an outward show of friendliness and sympathy in order to delude her victims. Both figures touch the young 'magician', they lure him to follow them.

Both women symbolise the inner struggle of man at the parting of the ways. At some point in our lifetime fate brings us all to this parting. We must choose whether we wish to go right or left. The right side leads us by way of difficult struggles involving even renunciation and sacrifices to a virtuous life, which nevertheless affords us a large measure of the pure joy of *true love*. The left side lures us to easy success without a struggle, to a licentious and profligate life, where we find short-lived pleasures in the gratification of our physical desire and urges. Such pleasures, however, inevitably leave a bitter after-taste and drag our consciousness irresistibly down to a lower level. The end of such a life is inner chaos and the destruction of the soul.

The two paths are symbolised by the two female figures. This does not mean, however, that *a man* at this parting of the ways must necessarily choose between *two women*. It can, of course, happen, but it would be only one instance among the many where a person, man or woman, stands before this fork. How often does it happen that for instance a doctor, a scientist, an artist or a businessman must choose between easy success, for which, however, he must sell himself and give up his inner conviction, and a hard life, which, while allowing him to act according to his conviction, denies him worldly success and material comfort. A Dr Hahnemann gave up his practice because he could not agree with the methods of treatment in use at that time. He preferred to let himself and his entire family go without food and to earn a meagre livelihood as a translator, rather than sell himself and his deepest conviction. Then he founded homeopathy and became world-famous! Yet what misery he and his family had to endure until that time! Or there is the case of a man like Böcklin to whom an art dealer promised a large sum of money if he would sentimentalise a straight-necked swan in one of his paintings by bending its neck in a rather mawkish manner. Böcklin thought of his starving family, hesitated for a moment, but then replied: 'No! I cannot do that. In this painting the swan holds himself erect!' And although the Böcklin family continued to live very frugally, Böcklin did not sell his conviction, his Self. Further examples worthy of mention are: Luther, who rejected the high ecclesiastical office offered him by the Pope as hush-money, preferring to let himself become the victim of religious persecution rather than betray his belief. Rembrandt suffered abject poverty and near starvation in order to explore the secrets of light and shade, instead of portraying rich burghers' wives as beautiful women, which would have made him wealthy in no time.

Many people have experienced this parting of the ways in themselves and know what it means 'to sell oneself to the devil'. Jesus of Nazareth also experienced it in the wilderness with the tempting of the devil. He was promised the kingdoms of the world if he would renounce his faith, follow the devil and do all that he commanded. How many people have stood at that same parting of the ways and had to drive away the devil with the divine words 'Apage Satanas!' – 'Get thee behind me, Satan!'

Of course it does happen that a man at this level of consciousness actually must choose between two women – or a woman between two men. Or perhaps they must choose only between two ways of life. The emphasis here is on the question whether, on account of material profit, a man betrays his inner conviction, his inner divine voice, thus selling his divine Self, or whether he staunchly obeys his inner voice and follows his conviction. This means that he *does the will of God*! And the greatest happiness of all is when man is satisfied in and with himself, for it means nothing other than that GOD is satisfied with him!

In the picture the angel is about to shoot an arrow into the magician's heart. He knows very well that the magician *can* and *will necessarily* choose *only* the right path. For whatever path he chooses, he will choose the right one *for himself*, because both paths will lead him to the same goal, to GOD. It is only a question of time, for the left one is slightly longer than the right one. For GOD, time does not exist. If the man is inexperienced, he will and *must* choose the left side, in order to make up for his lack of experience. On this left path he will realise that he makes himself unhappy, that he plunges into chaos and destruction of the soul. He loses himself on this path and falls out of unity, out of his divine SELF. And that is the greatest misfortune, that is hell. Thus he must turn back, 'become converted', and find the way out of this hell. He must strike the right path; now he has a rich store of experience. Then there will be no danger of his falling again. When Buddha suddenly realised after a night spent in his palace what a useless life he was leading, and how low it could drag him down, he went into seclusion to find GOD, to become BUDDHA.

Or another instance here in Europe: amidst a drunken rabble Francis of Assisi came to an understanding of himself and realised what he was actually doing. He rose and left never to return, to become the great saint, Francis.

Thus on the left path man must sooner or later awaken so that he will never again stray on to it believing that happiness is to be found there. He must find the right path and advance along it in order to reach the great goal. Each one of us must have this experience on the left path behind him, if he does not wish to stumble on the right path. For if he chooses the right side directly, *without the necessary experience*, he will be unable to resist the devil whenever he tempts him in the guise of some everyday trial. He lacks the power of experience and falls. Therefore he must go back to the left path to gather experience. If, however, someone brings this experience from previous lives, he can, and will choose the right path. If he still lacks experience he will choose, *with a deviation* to the left, the right path – if he is experienced, he will choose the right path *without deviation*.

The angel who plays the part of the sun, shoots the arrow – a ray of light – into the magician's heart. Thereupon he selects that path, which, in the light of his experience, will lead him to the goal, to GOD.

The tarot card THE PARTING OF THE WAYS carries the number 6 and the letter VAU.

The number 6 results from the two triangles joined to form a whole: one triangle lies with its point facing upwards, the other with its point downwards. The former symbolises the Holy Trinity, the latter, the resistance, the material world. If we unite the centres of the two triangles in one point, we get a six-pointed star which symbolises the human heart. In the heart into which the angel shoots his arrow, the two worlds, the spiritual and the earthly, meet. Man must realise both of them. In the spirit, the heavenly world, and in the body, the earthly one.

Tarot card 6, THE PARTING OF THE WAYS, finds its complement in tarot card 1, the MAGICIAN. Together they add up to the number 7, which again, as with the previous cards, leads to the number 10 by numerological reduction.

The letter VAU means the eye, therefore everything that

refers to light and brightness. The eye forms a bridge between man and the external world, for through the eye light and the outer world are revealed to him. The latter corresponds to the sixth *sefirah, Tifereth,* which means the sun and radiance, therefore everything that we see with our eyes.

THE CHARIOT

Number: 7

Letter: ⟩ ZAIN

In this picture we again meet the 'magician'. This time, however, he is no longer in a dilemma as on tarot card 6, nor does
he need to shield himself against alien influences as at the
'parting of the ways'. Now he stands self-assured and resolute,
not on foot, but in a cube-shaped chariot which hastens his
progress to the goal. At the turning-point of his life, at the
parting, he chose the right side – as we have shown, he could
choose *only* the right path – and he became conqueror.

He now wears a crown with three large shining stars. A
star radiates light and, as a symbol of light, it invariably stands
for consciousness. The three stars denote in this case the three
temporal phases of consciousness: past, present and future.
For these three phases of time exist only in man's conscious
mind. The conqueror has now reached the stage where he can
consciously build his future from the treasures of the past.

He wears a coat of mail. Its colour shows that he has a
spiritual outlook and deep belief in God. He wears a short
skirt on which we see three large yellow circles. The three
points of the skirt where the circles are placed are trimmed
with yellow. The three large circles symbolise the three worlds,
heaven, earth and hell, which he has already perceived to be

states of consciousness. The yellow border again denotes that he manifests his spirituality through his brilliant intellect.

On his chest we see a broad blue band on which are sewn the five buttons he already had as a 'magician'. These are again the five sense-organs linking him with the external world. In his right hand he holds his magic wand which, since he is now a conqueror, has become a mighty sceptre. He has become a ruler in his world.

On his shoulders we see the two celestial bodies, sun and moon, which we have already seen on the chest of the king of heaven. Man, as conqueror, is also in possession of the two great forces, the positive power of the sun and the negative power of the moon, and he quite consciously works with both of these creative energies.

The cube-shaped chariot reminds us of the throne of the ruler of heaven. Then, however, it was not a chariot but a simple cube. Now the conqueror uses this cube as a chariot for his triumphal procession. At each of the four corners of the chariot is a pole supporting a blue canopy above the head of the conqueror. The four poles symbolise the four elements: fire, air, water and earth. The conqueror stands between these poles at the point of intersection of the diagonals, thus uniting these four elements in himself and controlling them. The canopy consists of four large blue semi-circles. Each of these bears three stars, thus altogether there are twelve. These stand for the twelve signs of the zodiac as in the picture of the queen of heaven.

Some curious shapes are depicted on the front of the chariot. In the centre we recognise the two human sexual organs united. They rest within each other like the positive and the negative pole at the seventh level of consciousness. The Bible says: 'And on the seventh day God ended his work which he had made; and he rested on the seventh "day" from all his work which he had made.' (Genesis 2:2–3) In the Bible 'day' means consciousness and 'night' the unconscious. And the number 7 is the number of this card. The sacred philosophy of China represents this divine, neutral state of the two poles 'resting within themselves' by Yang and Yin.

This representation of the sexual organs in the picture is framed by a narrow oval yellow band. We understand from this that the conqueror who chose the right path on the sixth tarot card already knows intuitively as well as intellectually that the two sexes are in fact but one. They are the two halves of the divine WHOLE. Man, as a spiritual being, should therefore unite the two halves in himself at a high level of consciousness if he wants to be the 'whole'. In the body he can belong to the positive or the negative pole; in the spirit he contains both these poles and is androgynous. What is in his head, however – *what he understands* – is still far from realisation. Yet realisation has to begin with understanding. Then that which has been understood filters out of the intellect into the being. John says: 'And the Word was made flesh'; thus we gradually become that which previously we had merely understood. The person at this level of consciousness understands the unity of the two halves, but he is *still only one half* and not the WHOLE. He does not yet experience the WHOLE in a state of being.

Above this figure we recognise the Egyptian symbol of Logos, of the creative principle, which races through the universe creating and animating all things. It is the simplified shape of the Horus falcon, a red circle with large wings on either side. Therefore the spirit stands above separations: it is a unity. And the man who has fought his way up to this spiritual level is also a unity in his consciousness. In his spirit he is a WHOLE. A white and a black sphinx draw the chariot. We are familiar with the black sphinx from tarot card 2. There she was seated next to the high priestess's throne. The white sphinx was then still invisible. At the level of consciousness of the high priestess man knew only the material world and the laws of that world. Now he already knows both sides, the right and the left, the spiritual and the material world. They are no longer mysteries to him. If we examine the two sphinxes, we realise that they are not two sphinxes at all, but *one* sphinx with two torsos. The material-earthly world is the opposite image to the spiritual-divine world. What I *see* and what I *am* are always diametrically opposed. If we stand opposite someone, we see his right hand on the side of our left hand and at the same time his left hand on the side of our right hand. Therefore, what I *see*, I cannot *be*, and what I *am*, I cannot *see*. No artist can paint his self-portrait, for he can never see himself. He can see and paint only his reflected image. Yet that is not himself, it is not how he is in reality. His right side is on the left, and his left side is on the right side of the reflection!

This is true of everything, but for the moment we shall confine our attention to the example of writing only. When I look at the letter E it stands from left to right. If, however, I experience this same letter in a state of being, that is to say, if I write this E on my body *so that I am this E*, then it stands in reverse position, from right to left. In our modern Western culture, after the fall from Paradise, we read and write from left to right. Yet there are still peoples who have preserved their style of writing from primeval times, from a state of being, and who read and write from right to left. The Jews are such a nation. They transmit the state of being to the paper and read and write from right to left.

The white sphinx symbolises the state of being and the black sphinx the state of the fall from Paradise. They try to go in opposite directions, but in so doing achieve only the onward movement of the chariot as the resultant of the opposed energies.

The conqueror understands this truth and he *sees* and *is* the two sphinxes. He already knows the difference between the fallen state and the divine state of being, even if he is not yet always able to hold out in that state. He still falls, he projects himself again and again outwardly. Human frailty still draws him out of it; he has not yet been able to conquer it entirely. Nevertheless, he is on the homeward path. Just as the conqueror stands self-assured and self-confident in his chariot, so at this level man also acquires these characteristics. He begins to know his own powers, but he has already reached the stage where he knows, and does not forget, that all these powers are not his but belong to God. He now knows that without GOD he is nothing, that he receives all his abilities and talents from the single primal source of all powers. Everything that lives merely receives vital energy, abilities and talents. Michelangelo, Beethoven and other titans did not derive these powers from themselves; they all received them from God.

Man does not possess his *own* vital energy, abilities and talents. He obtains everything from God. Once he realises that, he loses his previous arrogance and egocentric perspective which could only grow from his ignorance, and he becomes modest. He knows that he is only the person, only a loudspeaker of God. In antiquity, 'persona' was the name given to the mask worn by players to let their voices 'come through'. Man lets God's voice come through himself. At the same time, however, he begins to feel that GOD loves and guides him, because GOD still has plans for him. For that very reason GOD bestows upon him abilities and talents, because HE intends to use him as a chosen instrument of manifestation. Man feels then that he is a child of God and always tries to do His will. He already knows that self-confidence is confidence in God! He knows that what is good in himself is GOD, and that what is imperfect in him is so because now and then he manifests his person and not GOD. He therefore tries to develop still further in order to become an even more effective loudspeaker of God. The greater his awareness of the futility of his person, the greater his self-confidence, because he feels that he is only the 'persona', the 'mask' of God, and that God speaks, instructs and loves all men through him. Thus he becomes an ever more efficient bearer of the divine powers. He notices that his words and deeds acquire a suggestive power over his fellow-men.

He uses this power to help others. People notice his superiority. Whatever he desires in his higher Self, he is able to carry out. He becomes a conqueror everywhere.

This time is a triumphal procession for man. He has won the great struggle at the parting of the ways. Now there are no more struggles and he cannot imagine that more and much harder struggles might be in store for him in the future. At this stage he rests on his laurels and believes that from now on the path will always lead upwards without great exertions on his part. He is satisfied with himself and with the world. He sees everything in an optimistic light and his fortune, too, brings him wide recognition and honour. Those people who do not yet know the vital sources from which he draws his energy admire him. They become his friends and want to learn from him. The difference between him and average men is not yet so great that they cannot understand him. Thus he is successful with his teachings and, in addition to his professional work, he takes time to occupy himself with his fellow-men. Everywhere he reaps recognition, love and honour.

Thus at this level man ends the first cycle of his development which is represented by the first seven tarot cards. At the same time, however, this level is also the beginning of a new cycle which starts with card 7 and ends with card 13. At this level of consciousness, therefore, man is at the end of the past and at the beginning of the future cycle of his development.

The tarot card 7 carries the number 7 and the letter ZAIN.

The number 7 is the most important number at our earthly level. Everything that is a unity here on earth breaks up into seven components. The Bible says that the seven souls of God animate the world and that the Creation consists of seven spheres of creation. In the Revelation of St John we read that the Lamb, the creative principle, Logos, has seven horns, which symbolise the seven creative powers. In the Cabbala and in the Indian Vedanta philosophy we find the same assertions and the seven levels are listed in the same manner: the material-physical, the vegetative, the animal, the mental, the causal, the divine-spiritual and the divine-creative. One of the greatest initiates of the West, Paracelsus, asserted the same truth. The highest product of creation on earth – man – consists of seven levels. Countryfolk have a saying: 'Man has seven skins.' The Bible lists many more instances: the seven fat cows and the seven lean cows denote the seven fat years and the seven lean years. And in heaven God gave a sign of his covenant with Noah: the rainbow made up of seven colours. The seven intervals of an octave; the seven vertebral bones of the human neck, of the giraffe or the mole; the seven hills on which Rome was built and the seven heads of the dragon in fairy-tales are all evidence of the great truth that the key number of the material world is 7.

Geometry also reveals the importance of the number 7. Every circle contains 7 smaller circles whose diameter measures exactly one third of the diameter of the large circle:

And in the three dimensions the number 7 is most significant: if the non-dimensional point moves from the unmanifested into manifestation, becoming a line in the first dimension, it contains three factors – the point of origin, the terminal point and the interval between the two. If the line continues to manifest itself with the same energy and speed in the second dimension, the area is created – the square with five factors. It has four sides and, as the fifth factor, the inner area. If the area continues to manifest itself in the third dimension, the cube is created with its seven factors: with six areas and the seventh factor, the volume. The number 7 is therefore the key number of the three-dimensional world. John, too, speaks in Revelation of the new holy Jerusalem, which is the Lamb's wife. 'And the city lieth foursquare, and the length is as large as the breadth: and he measured the city with the reed, twelve thousand furlongs. *The length and the breadth and the height of it are equal.*' (Rev. 21: 16) Thus we see that the new Jerusalem is a *cube*!

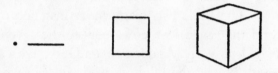

The number 7 also has a special relationship to the letters of the alphabet. If we mark the circumference of a circle with seven equidistant points, and join these up without retracing a line, we obtain exactly twenty-one links with the centre, therefore twenty-two factors. And our alphabet comprises exactly twenty-two letters with the letter Jay in the middle. The compound letters are merely further variations and not independent letters.

The letter ZAIN means: 'victory in all worlds'. It corresponds to the seventh *sefirah*, *Netsah*, which means endurance.

JUSTICE

Number: 8

Letter: ח CHETH

Here again we see the queen of heaven in new attire and with different attributes. She still wears her crown but under it is a red cap. This shows that she now has to work very hard with her spirit. She penetrates everything with the power of the spirit in order to be just. The circle on the cap with the dot in the centre is the symbol of self-confidence. Now the queen of heaven has no wings. She does not need them; she no longer flies in boundless heaven but has climbed down to earth – into the world of activity – in order to dispense justice.

She is seated upon a mighty throne which provides her with a stable basis. On the back of the throne there are eight yellow buttons – four to the right and four to the left – on a red background. They symbolise the number 8, the number of this tarot card. The number is also formed by placing one of the round scales on top of the other.

Her attire is rich in colours. The upper part of her bodice is red with a white border, the lower part is blue, which is also the colour of the lower half of her sleeves. She wears a red skirt, and over it an azure cloak with a green lining draped on her knees. As we know, red is invariably the symbol of spirituality, and blue the symbol of pure faith. The white border stands for the manifestation of the spirit through purity, the green lining for sympathy and benevolence to all living creatures. The upper half of her sleeves is made of yellow and green stripes revealing that she acts with benevolent intentions and wisdom.

In her right hand she holds a long sword, developed from the earlier sceptre. She rules no longer with her sceptre but with the sword of strife. She needs a weapon with which to enforce her decisions and judgement irresistibly and immutably. She often has to dispose of weighty problems with her sword as Alexander the Great had done with the Gordian knot. At the same time this sword is the queen's power of discrimination enabling her to separate the sheep from the goats. The sword is the discernment with which justice, having weighed every thought, word and deed, distinguishes the right in man from the wrong, eliminating the latter from his nature. In her left hand the queen of heaven holds a pair of scales which she uses to weigh everything that enters her sphere. The great question is whether she finds a thing too heavy or too light, accordingly keeping it or letting it fall.

Having attained self-confidence at the level of the conqueror, man must finally, at the level of justice, establish order in his inner being. Until now he has directed his attention outwards and cast the impressions of life, without examining whether they were right or wrong, partly into his inner being, partly into his unconscious, as if into a large vessel. Now he has reached the stage where he must create order in himself. He fetches up memories from his unconscious to his conscious mind, and weighs the smallest impressions to find out whether they deserve to be absorbed or whether they must first be digested. He must create a balance for everything he bears within in order to find the absolute equilibrium in himself. If he discovers painful memories which still hurt him, he must find an explanation to balance out these memories so that he now sees them only as instructive experiences. He can even be pleased about them, because these painful experiences helped him to make great progress. He raises the image of all his friends and foes to his consciousness and tries to find out why he feels friendly towards one and hostile towards another. This kind of inner work can yield strange results. It was often precisely through his enemies rather than through his friends – who were perhaps not his *real* friends at all – that he learned and experienced and became more shrewd, prudent and wise. His enemies did not spare him, they often told him the objective truth to his face. His friends, on the other hand, did not want to hurt him and, purely out of false consideration and love, passed over his obvious mistakes in silence. Yet he will also find that he has had some real, true friends in his life, who also told him his mistakes or errors to his face, but nevertheless always stood by him. He now appreciates these true friends more than ever and will henceforth cherish them in his heart, in his grateful soul.

In the course of this work on himself in his inner being, something strange happens to him in the outer world. Previously, at the level of consciousness of tarot card 7, he was generally admired; many people came to him to ask his advice. Many came to question him about inner, spiritual matters. Many wanted to learn from him. Thus at that time he was like a magnet surrounded by seekers. Now that he has become uncompromising with himself as well as with others, the number of those who ask his advice, who want to hear his truths and learn from him, has significantly decreased. At the seventh level he had not yet learned discretion, nor did he know that one must not freely impart each and every truth to immature men. Thus many people found him hard, devoid of understanding and unfeeling. Instead of prudently keeping silence, he grew less forbearing and stated his views unsparingly. This uncompromising frankness caused a certain estrangement between himself and those who could not fully understand him and the motives for his actions. The more skilled he grew at distinguishing the right from the wrong, the fewer were those who admired him and who were always in agree-

ment with him. Of his once large circle there remained but a
few like-minded friends. In addition to this, he had weighed
up everything in himself, recognised and realised his previously unobserved mistakes. That is why he grew more
modest and felt less superior to others. Many had misunderstood this: his new modesty, growing out of his objectivity,
the very sign of his inner greatness, they exploited in order to
criticise and belittle him. Now, however, in his present state
of consciousness, recognition by others is no longer as important to him as it used to be. His vanity has dwindled to such
an extent that the approval of his inner voice, the voice of his
higher Self, has become much more important to him than the
acknowledgment and praise of the circle around him. Thus
he continues along the chosen path and goes on working *in*
and *on himself.*

Man therefore creates a general order within himself, tries
to weigh up everything correctly and to perceive the true
value of his experiences. He proceeds systematically and with
method, and out of the chaos which formerly prevailed in
him he establishes a divine order. He registers all his experiences up to the present time and allots to each of them its
proper place according to its true weight in his inner being.
All that he has ever done or left undone he subjects to a merci-
less reckoning. And he realises that he *should* have done many
things he did not do, and should *not* have done many things
he did do. He continues to weigh things up: 'That was the
right thing to do, but I should not have done that.' He makes
an irrevocable decision: 'Next time I shall do everything much,
much better! May God grant me the opportunity to do so!'

Tarot card 8 carries the number 8 and the letter CHETH.

The number 8 is the self-reflecting and thereby self-dupli-
cating divine circle, the symbol of the eternal spirit. If we
place the circle on a mirror, we see the number 8. The spirit,
the only absolute reality, is reflected in the material world of
visions. It manifests itself in the material, subjectively real,
and therefore transient, world. In Creation this process is

without beginning or end, it is endless, and for that reason mathematicians have chosen this sign as the symbol of infinity. They draw it in a horizontal position so that we know it is not an ordinary 8. Just as the 8 runs on in itself from one circle over into another and in the same direction into infinity, so man circles out of his unconscious into consciousness, bringing out of the former into the latter long-since-forgotten and possibly repressed experiences. He weighs up the retrieved experiences, registers and judges them, until, out of the chaos, he has created order in his inner being. He learns that everything he apparently experiences in the external world, thus his entire fate, does not come from outside but exists within himself. If he does not like his fate, then he must change himself. Fate will then let him experience those things he will like.

In Greek mythology we are told the beautiful story of Narcissus. He caught sight of himself in the reflecting water and since he did not know that he himself was this beautiful image, he returned time and again to the water to look at the handsome stranger. Thus it is with man and his fate in the external world. He does not know that it is only a reflection of his Self, of his spirit. Therefore: the number 8 is the reflection of the eternal spirit in the world of visions, in the imaginary world, in the material world.

In the Cabbala, the letter CHETH corresponds to the eighth *sefirah*: *Hod* means praise and splendour.

Tarot Card 9

THE HERMIT

Number: 9

Letter: ט TETH

Having created inner order out of the chaos and arranged all the real and false values in his inner being in their proper order, man withdraws from the 'fata morgana' of this world and becomes a recluse. However, this does not indicate by any means that at this level of consciousness he actually withdraws to a lonely cave. The picture is merely a symbolic representation of his inner state, but not of his outward appearance in the world of visions. He continues to fulfil his duties at work and in everyday life, to wear conventional clothes and to behave as his fellow-men behave.

In the picture we see a man who, with his white beard and moustache, shows that he has finished with all outward appearances and above all has completely renounced vanity.

To those who behold him only from the outside, the hermit shows his dark grey cloak which, when he uses the hood, covers even his head. This cloak, however, is lined in a beautiful azure blue. This reveals that underneath the colourless manifestation and his drab outward appearance, he has a very deep, true belief in God. Under the cloak he wears an orange-coloured robe. Orange results from mixing red and yellow, spirituality and intelligence, which together constitute divine wisdom. In his inmost being there no longer exists any earthly quality; he has grown wise and all feelings of sympathy or antipathy, love or aversion, are dominated by his divine wisdom.

In his left hand he holds a stick; it is not a magic wand with which he could work miracles, nor is it a sceptre, symbol of rulership, nor a sword, symbol of courage and the power of discrimination; it is a simple walking-stick which helps him to make progress.

In his right hand he holds aloft a simple lantern. It is nothing other than the light of his intellect with which he illumines his path in the darkness in order not to lose his way. He holds the lantern in such a manner that he alone sees its light. He hides the small lamp from the eyes of others with his loose cloak. Formerly, he passed on all the fresh insights and truths he had found himself to other seekers. He slowly began to realize, however, that few people understood him and that it was best if he kept his newly discovered truths for himself. Therefore he no longer freely shows the light of his intellect and knowledge to other people, only to his intimate friends. He has learned *to keep silence*!

Before him, on the ground, we see a strange creature, a small monster. It is red in colour and thus denotes a spiritual manifestation. It symbolises man's healthy instincts which act from his unconscious and with the help of his reason lead him unerringly to the right path. These instincts cause the strange 'coincidences' in his life which invariably indicate exactly the direction he should take, the people he should trust or distrust and with whom he should associate only with the greatest caution, if he must associate with shady characters at all. This small monster, his healthy instincts, will always put into his hands just the right books where he may find the truths to guide him to maturity; it will also enable him to hear the voice of God through the tongues of man. This small monster saves him a great deal of unnecessary wandering about and unerringly leads him ever closer to the great goal. One day he also recognises *himself* in this creature, in his own instincts.

When man has reached this level of consciousness, he suddenly feels the urge to leave everything and to go away. He has perceived that the value of the affairs of this world lies only in what he may learn from them. Yet once he knows the goal we have ultimately to attain, why should he then still continue to participate in the affairs of this world? His professional work no longer offers him satisfaction, indeed it suddenly appears to him futile and useless. Why then go on? He already knows that family relationships and ties of friendship are transient and last only as long as he remains in this world.

When the time comes for him to leave earthly things behind, he takes with him only that which is eternal. All things pass, only one thing remains: true spiritual togetherness and love. But that, too, he can take with him even if, while still in this life, he leaves everything behind and goes away. He finds everything here a burden, he does not want to waste any more time, he would like to live only for the essence of life and to work only in and on himself, in order to experience unity with GOD. In other words he would like to go away! – Yes! But where? – To Tibet – or now that Tibet is out of the question for this purpose, to India, or Athos, the legendary Greek monastery? Deep down inside he is seized by an irresistible longing to be free, free from all that ties and enslaves him. And he already begins secretly to make plans. He tries to imagine what it will be like if he goes away – leaves here and arrives – but where? – It is so easy to imagine *leaving*, but that implies at the same time that one *must* also *arrive* somewhere! And where will that be, where will he arrive and how? A monastery? – Will he be able to be free there? – No! There he will really have to obey blindly, even more than before, and what is more, he may have one or more superiors who belong to another world, who are total strangers to him and completely unable to understand him. He has to keep company with people he does not like and who may have highly unpleasant habits. And he must keep quiet and obey, whether he likes it or not.

If he does not enter a monastery, but behaves like the Indians who lead a nomadic existence or retreat to a cave, what then? – What will he eat, for eat he must. Will he go begging? No, definitely not! He could, however, work somewhere, make himself useful, perhaps with lepers? He certainly could, and indeed many try it, but many more know in advance what he already knows too, namely, that out there in Asia he will be even more enslaved than before. He would have still less chance of living for what he would like to live for, than if he were simply to stay at home where the milkman comes every day and his home exudes the warmth of central heating. And if furthermore he has a family, yet still goes away, he will have such a guilty conscience about these loved ones that he will never be able to forgive himself. How then could he feel free? Therefore, the very best thing will be if he stays at home and, instead of tending lepers, adopts the same attitude of self-sacrifice which would have been necessary for that task, continuing to fulfil his own duties at work with full concentration and devotion. And thus man arrives at the truth that this 'going away' which he sought, should take place not in the external world, but in himself. He wants to and must escape from himself, from his own inner perspective and inner enslavement. He is not enslaved by other people, but by himself. For if he feels enslaved here, he will take this feeling wherever he may go. If, however, he feels free in the midst of his family and at work, then he will take this freedom wherever he may go. What is the point then in going away? He knows that there have been many people who actually did 'go away', who really lived in a Tibetan or Indian monastery or with a great master. Yet they found exactly the same truths in those places as they can find here, in their present surroundings, if only they are ready for them. God leads men on different paths, but on each of these individual paths we all attain exactly the same great goal: GOD!

We see, therefore, that it is the destiny of such a man, as yet, not to walk away from everything. Thus he remains where he is and tries *inwardly* to break away from his surroundings and his personal world and to obtain *inner* liberation.

And his dress? – Oh! How he has longed to be free of fashion, from vain outward appearances! For he realises that what we wear is of no importance. One can be a hermit and yet wear the same clothes as other people. In a monastery, too, one has to wear the regulation clothes like the other monks – therefore also conform to 'fashion'! And what about the Indians who do not live in a monastery? – We can be free of all these things, whether wearing European dress or wandering down a main road in India clad in rags, if we are inwardly free from them. For instance, if a young woman is a *true* nun in her being, she can even attend balls in a low-necked evening dress yet be a true recluse, because she is *so in herself.* And likewise a man can dress fashionably, join in the laughter of others and yet be a true monk *in himself.*

At this level of consciousness man therefore withdraws into himself, continues to work on himself and tries to break away and find release from everything. He renounces the importance of his person, he renounces ambition and no longer seeks to draw attention to himself in the external world or to get ahead in his profession; or at least he does not make it any kind of end in itself. As man or woman he tries to perform his tasks as he would have done in the place he wanted to visit in his imagination. Now he does not work for himself, but *for the sake of work.* In the course of this he experiences unsuspected and unhoped-for new joys. Work begins to become an end in itself for him. He works no longer to earn success and praise or to make a lot of money, but in order to achieve perfection.

Meanwhile, he completely forgets himself and all his troubles; in concentrating on his work he forgets all the disappointments of his life and all that has hurt him in the past. He discovers that he has become free through nothing other than work alone, and he experiences great self-transcending joys. Now he understands why Asian as well as European monks and nuns have to work in their communities. In the garden, in the kitchen or in the library, they have to work for the sake of work, in order to become free through work. But we can do that at home, too; we do not need to leave our family and friends for that.

The ninth tarot card carries the number 9 and the letter TETH.

In numerology the meaning of the number 9 is absolute passivity. Thus the hermit is also completely passive within himself. He has become totally detached and does not participate in worldly activities. If he performs his everyday duties at this level of consciousness, his motives are utterly unselfish.

The number 9 has several strange qualities. For instance, if we add it to another number, whether high or low, this will not change the sum of the digits. Let us take as our first example the low number 17. The sum of the digits is 8. If we add 9 to 17 the result is 26. Again, the sum of the digits is 8. Now let us take the higher number 435. The sum of the digits is 12, by numerological reduction, 3. If we now add 9 to 435, the result is 444. The sum of the digits is again 12 and 3 respectively. If we add any number to the number 9, the sum of the digits always remains constant. The number 9 shows another strange characteristic if we conduct the following experiment: make a vertical list of the numbers from 0 to 9. Now list the same sequence of numbers in reverse and put the two rows together:

0	9	09
1	8	18
2	7	27
3	6	36
4	5	45
5	4	54
6	3	63
7	2	72
8	1	81
9	0	90

What have we obtained? The result of the multiplication of the number 9 from one to ten. And if we add these numbers together the sum of the digits is invariably the number 9:

$$
\begin{aligned}
\text{Thus:} \quad 1 \times 9 &= 9 = 9 \\
2 \times 9 &= 18 = 9 \\
3 \times 9 &= 27 = 9 \\
4 \times 9 &= 36 = 9 \\
5 \times 9 &= 45 = 9 \\
6 \times 9 &= 54 = 9 \\
7 \times 9 &= 63 = 9 \\
8 \times 9 &= 72 = 9 \\
9 \times 9 &= 81 = 9 \\
10 \times 9 &= 90 = 9
\end{aligned}
$$

And yet another highly interesting quality of this number: make a vertical list of numbers starting each time with 1 and add the next number in each consecutive row. If we multiply these numbers by 9 and add the numbers from 1 to 10 to each sequence, we obtain the following strange results:

$$
\begin{aligned}
0 \times 9 + 1 &= 1 \\
1 \times 9 + 2 &= 11 \\
12 \times 9 + 3 &= 111 \\
123 \times 9 + 4 &= 1111 \\
1234 \times 9 + 5 &= 11111 \\
12345 \times 9 + 6 &= 111111 \\
123456 \times 9 + 7 &= 1111111 \\
1234567 \times 9 + 8 &= 11111111 \\
12345678 \times 9 + 9 &= 111111111 \\
123456789 \times 9 + 10 &= 1111111111
\end{aligned}
$$

I could mention further very interesting characteristics of the number 9, but that would lead us away from our subject. I merely wished to show that the number 9 is an unusually interesting and significant number. It destroys itself, yet continues to exist. With such qualities this number corresponds exactly to the level of consciousness of the 'hermit', because it invariably remains itself. If anyone takes these remarkable characteristics of the number 9 as a matter of course, he is advised to try these experiments with another number. He will then see the great difference between the numbers.

In hieroglyphics the letter TETH represents the idea of protection and safety. TETH denotes the guardian angels who guide men from their birth onwards. It corresponds to the ninth *sefirah*, *Yesod*, which means foundation, wisdom.

THE WHEEL OF FORTUNE

Number: 10

Letter: ' YOD

In this picture we see a strange wheel in a small boat afloat on the waves. The boat consists of two half-moons, one is positive-red, the other negative-green. A sturdy grey pole stands in the boat and round its base coil two serpents, one positive-red, the other negative-green. A large wheel is attached to the top of the pole. At the point where the wheel is fixed to the pole, thus on the axis of the wheel, there is a handle. From this we see that the wheel is being turned. The wheel consists of two circles: the outer, larger one is red, the inner, smaller one, blue. The red one signifies spirituality, the blue one, deep faith in God. The spokes of the wheel are yellow, therefore the two wheels are sustained by intelligence and intellectual powers.

Two strange creatures cling to the wheel. One of them looks like an animal, a dog with a human body. Its head and long mane are yellow, its body is blue. It wears a yellow sash round its belly, the loose part of it fluttering out behind him. In its hand it holds the 'Hermes staff'.

The other creature on the wheel is a devil with a Neptune's trident in his hand. Instead of feet, he has fins like a Triton. This shows that he is connected with the element 'water'. His head is a nondescript dark colour, his body is green. He, too,

THE WHEEL OF FORTUNE

wears a sash round his belly: its colour matches his head and
the loose part flutters out behind him. From this part of the
sash we see that the wheel is being turned in an anti-clockwise
direction by some invisible agent.

Above the wheel a sphinx sits on a yellow board. In her,
all four elements are represented. Her head is red, her head-
dress red and white-striped. Therefore her head belongs to the
element 'fire'. Her wings are blue and thus denote the element
'air'. She has the body of a lion; the upper part is green and
belongs to the element 'water'; the lower part is brown and
belongs to the element 'earth'. The tip of her tail is red like
her head, thus again fiery. The sphinx has lions' paws; in her
right front paw she holds a short sword.

What does this strange picture mean?

It shows the human state of consciousness following upon
the ninth level of consciousness, symbolised by the picture
'Hermit', where, in his inmost being, man withdraws from
the 'world' and breaks away from all his personal concerns.
It is only outwardly that he plays his part in the ups and downs
of life, inwardly he is serene and free. Not without a hard
struggle he has cut himself off not only from the 'world', but
also from his entire destiny. He now knows that he cannot
run away from the problems he has to solve because they go
with him. He would take the problems with him and acquire
new ones in addition, which would always demand the same
answer of him. Now he has reached the stage where he sheds
all his inescapable problems as a snake sheds its skin. The
answer, therefore, to his outward destiny in this world was not
to leave his family and work, but rather, to learn and gain
experience from these. Thus he had to cope with all the difficulties of life from which he would have liked so much to
escape. When he has learned what he had to learn, he will
have new and more sophisticated work and more intricate
problems to solve, in order to learn yet further truths
and gain fresh experience. Now he no longer wants to run
away from his present situation, work and duties but to learn

as much as possible from them. He consciously looks for what these circumstances can still teach him and what spiritual and intellectual advantage he may derive from them. In the course of this he does not notice that a gradual change is taking place around him because, in the first instance, it does not occur from the outside, but in himself. His *reaction* to everything that happens to him has changed. In his inner world he is a true *hermit*.

In the external world no one notices anything of this. Things are still the same, his life seems to continue as before. For the time being, the difference is that he begins to look at everything, his whole life on earth, from above, just as the sphinx looks down on everything. He continues to free himself inwardly from all that has tied him in the past and allows his person to act like an implement without himself being touched by it. He perceives the solutions of his problems only rationally, he does not participate in them heart and soul. He regards all his affairs as if they belonged to a third party. He remains in a superior position like the sphinx above the wheel of fortune, who symbolises his higher Self and looks on impartially at what happens. She holds the sword in her 'paw', ready to strike and obtain what she wants if anything should happen against her will.

In this state of consciousness man no longer swims himself in the ocean of life, but lets himself be carried along on the waves in a boat. In the picture this boat consists of two half-moons. As in the picture of the queen of heaven, the moon stands for man's emotions. He has already become spiritual, loving and understanding. This is shown by the red and green of the half-moons. The red and blue circles also denote that he judges things first from an intellectual and only afterwards from an emotional point of view. The yellow spokes stand for the powers of intellect, which dominate in his present state.

The vertical pole supporting the wheel of fortune and the two serpents coiling round it are nothing else but an extended Hermes staff, the symbol of man, going back to the great

Chaldean mystic, Hermes Trismegistos. This staff, as depicted in the hand of the creature, has two wings at the top and is surmounted by a small ball. The staff symbolises the human spine, the ball denotes man's reason, and the two wings his spirit hovering up above. Two serpents twine round the staff. They cross at several points and keep each other in check. There is tension between them. The serpents symbolise the two great vital currents in man. In the Indian Vedanta philosophy they are known as the two main channels of life: Ida and Pingala Nadi. Pingala, the red serpent, passes on the right side, Ida, the green serpent, on the left side of the spine. The central canal in the spine is called Sushumna Nadi. The wheel in the picture signifies man's fate, which he himself has shaped and which revolves around his Self like the planets around the sun. His two great instincts revolve with his earthly-material person. These are the instinct of self-preservation and the instinct of preservation of the species, over which he has not yet attained complete mastery. The instinct of self-preservation is symbolised in the picture by an animal, since it is the 'animal in us', as Paracelsus termed it. This controls our mortal bodies and thus, too, our physical health. That is why the animal creature holds the Hermes staff with the three currents of life. This instinct governs the body from within and endows us with the ability as well as the urge to keep our bodies healthy, to eat, drink and act in the interest of our health. This is true at least in the case of *healthy* people, if they have not yet destroyed their healthy instincts with various addictions.

The instinct of preservation of the species is symbolised in the picture by a devil who works with the body-fluids through which life is transmitted. This devil is here the symbol of the unconscious, sexual, purely animal instinct in man, which has nothing to do with love.

These two instincts are active only in the body, in our earthly person, but not in our spirit, since they are the physical manifestation of the spirit. The same thing cannot be in two places at once. Divine-creative power manifests itself either in the spirit as creative power, or in the body as sexual energy. At this level of consciousness man is already spiritually aware, but has not yet been able to convert the two instincts. Nevertheless, he already dominates them with his reason, just as the sphinx in the picture dominates everything and determines from above what should happen in the body, in one's own person. Man already rules in his realm. As the Upanishads so aptly put it:

> He who, dwelling in the earth, yet is other than the earth, whom the earth does not know, whose body the earth is, who controls the earth from within – He is your Soul, the Inner Controller, the Immortal.

As in the Bible, earth in this context means the body, the person composed of earthly powers. It does not know the spirit, the Self, the Immortal – but the spirit, the Self, the Immortal knows the Mortal, the person – and governs it from within, from the unconscious.

This card carries the number 10 and the letter YOD. (In our alphabet, I.)

The number 10 is the number of fulfilment, the perfection of creation. The boundless circle, the cipher, which at the same time forms the letter O, symbolises the universe, boundless space, the maternal aspect of God. In itself it is the absolute nothingness that is ready, however, to give birth to everything and to take it all back again and absorb it into itself. The cipher becomes a number only when it is preceded by any of the other nine numbers. The number one and the letter YOD (our I) are identical. They are the first original manifestation of God. All ensuing numbers and letters originate from this primal festation. It is the fecundity of God, Logos, the creative principle which creates countless worlds and living creatures in the great and boundless cipher, in infinite space. In the number 10 creation reaches perfection and fulfilment. The masculine-positive, creative principle of God has penetrated and fertilised space, the negative, maternal aspect, and has become one with it.

The number 10, correctly depicted, is a circle containing the fertilising, positive-creative power of God:

The picture of the wheel of fortune also represents the number 10. The wheel is the cipher and the pole supporting the wheel is the number 1. This number 1 is, however, identical with the letter YOD or I.

In the Hebrew alphabet, as in every other, all the letters derive from the one YOD or I. Hebrew letters are letters of fire. Each character is a combination of flames. *Yod* is the very first flame of the divine fire, of the spirit of God. All other flame formations – the letters – proceed from this first flame. Just as the number one is the first number from which all further numbers spring forth, so the letter *yod* is the first letter, the first flame from the spirit God, from which all further letters are derived and formed. At the level of consciousness of the wheel of fortune man must penetrate to the depths, the roots of his being, from where, endowed with a new perspective, he must find a new direction and follow a new path. Just as on tarot card 1 the 'Magician' with the number one and the letter *aleph* was the beginning, so now, at the level of the wheel of fortune, at which the number one is linked with the boundless cipher, he will again be the beginning at a higher level. From now on he will no longer move in single figures, but coupled with the cipher, symbol of the universe, he will advance by ten at a time. Now he is not an isolated, personal being, but begins to become a part of the universe – hence the cipher.

The tenth *sefirah* is *Malkhuth* and means kingdom. This tarot card marks the end of the *sefiroth* sequence.

Tarot card 10 complements tarot card 9. Together they make 19, which by cabbalistic reduction again leads to the number 1 : 10+9 = 19, 1+9 = 10 = 1.

POWER

Numerical Value: 20

Letter: כ Kaph

Again we see the queen of heaven with her fair hair and golden crown. Now, however, her crown has five points. These symbolise the creative number of the Logos. Under her crown she wears a hat which, like the magician's hat, is really the sign used to denote infinity. This shows again that the POWER of the beautiful woman is infinite, that it is sustained by infinity. The right side of her hat is richly lined with golden laurel leaves as a sign of victory. The brim of the hat has a red border on the lower right extending all the way along on top. On the inner left side the border is green.

The yellow of the crown and of the inner side of the hat show that she manifests herself through her intelligence, through her reason. Her forearms are also yellow, therefore she acts with wisdom and not without goodwill and understanding. Her goodwill is shown by the green of the wide upper part of her sleeves and of the cuffs. She wears an azure dress with a red belt gathering it in and over it a full red cloak. The azure dress is the symbol of pure faith and trust in God. But faith and emotions are watched over and governed by the spirit. The full red cloak hanging loosely and open from the woman's shoulders symbolises the ever ready and alert spirit enveloping her whole being so that no one may see and perhaps unnecessarily exploit her gentle and loving inner nature.

Beside her is a mighty lion with huge paws. His mouth is wide open, because the woman's gentle hands open his jaws and hold them apart. The lion has strong teeth, but he cannot bite the woman's hands because she holds his mouth open with insuperable strength. She does not even have to exert herself. She has such great strength that she controls the mighty lion easily and without effort.

What is the power that is so much greater than the strength of the mightiest of beasts?

This power, the strongest in the world, is the all-overwhelming, all-conquering power of LOVE.

The man who, to become superior like the sphinx, has struggled with his destiny at the tenth level of consciousness of the wheel of fortune has learned a great deal in this conflict – even things which were not really directly related to his destiny. Yet without these experiences he would never have been able to come to terms with his fate. He had to learn to be totally objective towards his fellow-men, to think and feel objectively, otherwise he would have been unable to solve his daily problems, even those of everyday life. But how could he suddenly have adopted an objective point of view? Only one method, but a very effective one, could lead him to this. He had to learn to *imagine himself in the place of his opponent,* thereby adopting and accepting the standpoint of the other person. Suddenly the whole matter appeared to him in an entirely different light. As a result he was no longer upset or worried about it. He considered the whole problem calmly and OBJECTIVELY and soon found the answer.

At first, this method of putting oneself in the other person's place was governed by reason. If anything happened to upset him, he consciously took a deep breath and thought something like this: 'Just keep calm, don't get excited! Let me try to put myself in the place of the person whose point of view I cannot at the moment accept, then we shall see where the truth lies, which of us is right.' And then, in his imagination, he really, quite consciously, 'changed places'. And behold, the objectivity was there at once, he could see the matter and reason it out from an objective viewpoint and settle the whole affair to everyone's satisfaction. Then, as time went by, he needed this rational approach less and less. He no longer had to take a deep breath to calm his frayed and fretting, ever-excitable nerves. Now they very quickly acquired the calm ordered by his reason. And when again a situation arose where he had to put himself in the other person's place, his method won him immediate success. He did not first have to calm himself and then become objective; he could remain composed from the start and there and then quietly take control of the situation. As a consequence of this, everyone around him admired him for his imperturbable composure and began to emulate it. People again came to seek his advice in all kinds of matters. But he has already learned to keep silent at the level of the 'Hermit'. Therefore he no longer reveals his high inner truths to immature men. He is also careful not to 'cast his pearls before swine', as it says in the Bible, but rather, in the words of the Apostle Paul, he has learned 'to speak with tongues'. He no longer wishes that people understand *him*, rather, *he* begins to understand *them*. He tries to speak with the tongues of others. And suddenly he notices that people begin to interest him, the way they live, how they shape their destiny. Interest in something, however, leads to affection for it. Yet this has not come about by an act of will. It has happened of its own accord, he has to admit that love is independent of our will. Either we love or we do not love. It does not depend on us. One day, whether he wanted to or not, he came to love his fellow-men. At first he had done so out of an inner urge and acted 'as if' out of love. Gradually, however, as his understanding for people grew, he could stop behaving 'as if' he acted out of love; instead, the love and the interest were really there. The strange thing is that he now recognises himself in each person, even in the most primitive man at the lowest level. He is now fully aware that he, too, was once just as primitive and low. In the struggles of others he has perceived his own initial conflicts and has been overcome by sympathy and understanding for his fellow-men. Through other people he has also gained in self-knowledge. Each person is like himself, each one is his own reflected image, often even his caricature, yet still essentially himself. Love is the inner urge for oneness and he begins to love men, animals, plants, the whole universe. He feels one with all living things. This love has nothing to do with the low level of love, sexuality. It exists only in the heart and has its source in spiritual oneness. This love is the greatest power in the world. Love is life, love is BEING. And eternal BEING is GOD.

Anyone who bears true love in his heart does not need to wear a constant smile on his face. Love is not sentimentality, nor a matter of 'feeling good'. Love never needs demonstration. Those of us who possess it will prove it by deeds, but we shall never *want* to prove it. Love must simply be THERE as the inner motive for our actions. The sun does not have to *will* the radiation of light and warmth; it simply radiates light and warmth. Thus the person who has reached the eleventh level of consciousness radiates love and warmth through which he conquers all living creatures, the whole world. Yes, even the king of animals, the mighty lion! We all know this lion from our dreams. As in dreams, the lion depicted here symbolises the great powers of the body and the two great instincts manifesting themselves through the body.

While the lion in this picture is already dominated, he is not yet fully vanquished. The beautiful woman still has to hold him, she must not let go. But the lion is already governed by the very strongest manifestation and power of the spirit, he is governed by LOVE.

Tarot card 11 carries the total of the digits of the number 11, thus the number 2, and the 0 symbolising boundless space, thus the number 20, and the letter KAPH. Until now we had only one-figure numbers. After the first ten we have double figures which are added together according to the cabbalistic method in order to obtain the sum of the digits. In the case of the number 11 it is 2, which can never occur in a unit. Like the number 2, the number 20 is also a duplication because the 0 does not count in cabbalistic reduction. And so *kaph* is also a double letter in the Hebrew alphabet.

The picture POWER illustrates two factors: the conqueror and the conquered. The conqueror is the beautiful woman, symbol of the greatest power, love. Her conquest is the lion, symbol of the two great instincts of the body and of its resistance against the spirit. We can also call these factors power and vitality. Both are equally important, but the power of the spirit, love, must govern the vitality of the body.

The letter KAPH corresponds to the name Chabir (the mighty one) and designates the 'first heaven' and the first cause, which sets in motion all that can be moved. The hieroglyphic meaning of the letter KAPH is the human hand as the concept of the firm grasp. Hence all ideas of power correspond to this letter.

THE HANGED MAN

Numerical Value: 30

Letter: ל LAMED

In this picture our magician appears once more. On the first card he stood at the beginning of the path, on the sixth card we saw him at the parting of the ways and on the seventh card as the conqueror who has mastered, and is in control of, his seven powers. In this picture we see him as a hanged man. Does this mean that he has lost ground again? Hardly, because he seems to be pleased with his situation. His face has a cheerful and happy expression. Let us therefore examine this picture thoroughly!

To the right and left are two tree-trunks; we again recognise the two pillars of Solomon, Jachin and Boaz. Each trunk had six branches which have been cut off. The stumps are still visible. The lower parts of the trunks are blue, the remainder green; the stumps are red. At the level where the seventh branch would have been, the two trunks were severed and a yellow plank was laid across them. The young man is suspended from this plank. A heavy rope has been tied round his left ankle fastening him to the plank. He holds his right leg so as to form a cross with his left leg. We recognise the same cross which the 'king of heaven' forms with his legs on tarot card 4. The hanged man wears dark brown shoes and blue hose. He wears a tunic of red and white material arranged so that the upper left side is white, the right side red, and below the yellow belt the colours are reversed. The two pockets shaped like half-moons and the six buttons on the tunic are red in the white part and white in the red part. His sleeves are yellow with red cuffs. He hides his green hands behind his back. Each arm supports a purse filled with money; one is pale blue, the other pale pink. He lets coins fall out of each purse: silver coins from the blue purse, gold from the pink one. His flaxen hair hangs down loosely.

This picture illustrates a very strange state which, for those who have not yet experienced it, is very difficult to understand. In this state man's way of seeing and doing things is diametrically opposed to that of the average person. And because he sees and does everything the other way round, he continuously comes into conflict with the world.

How does he come to see and do everything the other way round? Let us try to understand the picture! We shall then see that as soon as man has passed through all the levels previously described, he must inevitably and unavoidably reach this state.

He has climbed up the two trunks which have six levels. Therefore he had to get to know all six levels, the physical-material, the vegetative, the animal, the mental, the causal and the sixth, purely spiritual level. At this sixth level man no longer has his own will, he always performs the will of God. He hears the voice of God clearly within and knows what God asks of him; thus he has become an instrument of God. Hence it follows that in his highest spiritual state man speaks face to face with God like Moses 'on the mountain'. That is to say, his consciousness becomes identical with God, he merges into one state of being with God. The young magician has set foot on this seventh, highest level. As we see, his foot is still touching this seventh level, THUS HE STANDS ON IT, as it were, but *upside down*. In the language of mere common sense he is suspended from it.

He thus sees everything the other way round. How could it be otherwise when he has acquired true spiritual love at the level of tarot card 11 and looks at everything from the other person's angle, from the divine viewpoint of LOVE, of UNITY? And we know that the divine point of view and the human point of view are always the mirror reflections of each other.

These two tree-trunks reveal something else of great importance. The six branch knots and the seventh one where the trunk was cut off, show the seven spiritual centres of man which have their seat in the body in the most important nerve centres. These spiritual centres are known in the Indian Vedanta philosophy as 'chakras'. Yet we must never confuse these chakras with the nerve centres where they have their seat. A spiritual centre, thus a chakra, has the same relationship to the nerve centre where it rests, as the truck-driver to his truck. He sits inside, he sets it in motion and he steers it, but in no way is the driver his vehicle! Unfortunately, a great number of Western writers on the subject of the chakras do not know this difference between the chakras and the nerve centres and believe them to be one and the same thing. That is a great error. These spiritual centres, the chakras, have their seat in the bearer of life, in the spine. The lowest chakra in the spine, in the coccyx, sustains the negative pole. It is called the Muladhara chakra. The next chakra has its seat in the spine, below the region of the navel. It is called the Svadisthana chakra and governs potency. The third chakra sits in the solar plexus and is called the Manipura chakra. In the heart it is the Anahata chakra. The Vishuddha chakra has its seat in the thyroid gland; the Ajna chakra sits between the eyebrows; in the uppermost part of the skull is the highest chakra, seat of the positive pole. It serves to manifest the divine spirit and is called the Sahasrara chakra. These are the seven levels which man must reach. And when he has attained the seventh level where he wakens and activates the seventh chakra from its latent condition, he reaches the state where, like Moses, he may speak face to face with GOD. First, however, he must ascend the six levels, *activate* the six chakras.

The legs which have helped the young man to climb up are blue, the shoes brown. Wherever his steps may lead him, he will always be guided by true faith in God. He has become an instrument of God. He no longer possesses self-will. Only his shoes are brown, therefore only the lowest part of him, the soles of his feet, come into contact with matter, with the ground. He must stand on the ground as a basis! – His clothing is composed of various colours; white (purity), red (spirituality), yellow (intelligence) and green (goodwill). We already know the significance of this. In his heart he is spiritual and pure, in his activity he allows himself to be guided by his intelligence and reason. The white and red half-moons denote the negative lunar and the positive solar powers; he already has both of them 'in his pocket', that is to say, he is master of both of these powers. The six buttons which he now wears are the five sense organs and the sixth sense which he is now also very much in need of. Under his arms are two purses from which, because of his inverted position, his accumulated treasures can be seen falling to the ground, where they may be picked up by others. His treasures are gold, i.e. of positive-mental, and silver, i.e. of negative-spiritual nature. He passes on the fruits of his hard experiences to his fellow-men.

How could anyone with this outlook *fail* to see and do everything in the opposite way to average people who are still completely dominated by egoism, envy, greed and vanity? It is also quite natural that everything the 'hanged man' says or does is misunderstood and misinterpreted by ordinary men. He realises he has attained this level precisely because he is constantly misunderstood and time and again has to explain the reasons for his actions. Nor is this all. It is a strange fact that people who have reached this degree of development actually experience the state in which they feel as if they were suspended, without previous knowledge of the existence of this tarot card and state. Many dream of hanging like bats and many report that during meditation they suddenly feel lifted by the feet into the air and forced to stay in this position with the head hanging down. On opening their eyes they see that they are sitting in a normal position on the chair. This actually happens with practitioners of spiritual Yoga. Therefore it must be realised that the state in which we feel suspended upside down is connected with the expansion of consciousness. Experience shows that the man in the state of tarot card 12 not only thinks and acts in the spiritual sense in the opposite way to ordinary men, but that he also projects this spiritual state into the body, thereby experiencing it as a physical condition.

Here is an example of how a person thinks and acts from such an inverted position. Before leaving the house 'the hanged man' carefully locks his desk and all his cupboards. His servants and family think he does this because he is afraid someone might pry into his drawers during his absence. He locks everything up then, because he apparently suspects those around him. In actual fact, he does so for exactly the opposite reason: to protect those in his household from suspicion, so that if anything was missing from the drawers, or was not quite in order, no one, not even *himself*, would suspect – for the devil never sleeps – that any of these people had removed it. If he carefully locks everything, no one can possibly entertain such a thought or suspicion. Therefore, instead of suspecting those around him, *he shields them from any suspicion.* It seems hardly necessary to mention further instances. For the readers who have already reached or even advanced *beyond* this state of consciousness, will themselves discover, or have already done so, the truth of these statements. There is little point in discussing the matter with those who are still *below* this level. They will neither understand nor believe that such a thing is possible; they will think about it '*the wrong way round*'. The 'hanged men' are already accustomed to it.

It is amazing that the great initiates who created these pictures in order to represent the various states of consciousness knew the nature of man so intimately as to realise that this state is experienced not only mentally, but also, as a projection, physically. Many of those who have set foot upon the path already know these pictures. Yet they really only grasped their meaning and understood them when they suddenly and unexpectedly experienced these states themselves. Then the light dawned upon them and they humbly bowed before the initiates who had such deep psychological knowledge.

Tarot card 12, THE HANGED MAN, carries the total of the digits of the number 12, thus 3, linked with the 0, symbol of boundless space, thus 30; it also carries the letter LAMED.

The number 12 and all its multiples are the most significant numbers in the entire sequence of numbers. It is remarkable that a comparatively low number such as the number 12 is divisible by *six* numbers – thus by *half* of the numbers it contains! If we add these six numbers: $1+2+3+4+6+12$, we get the number 28, of which the sum of the digits is once again 10, the number of the perfection and fulfilment of creation. If we multiply the number of the Holy Trinity, 3, by that of the four faces of God, 4, we obtain the number 12, this unique number which is divisible by as many as half of the numbers of its own value. With no other number is this possible, not even with the highest numbers. Mankind has recognised the importance of this number from time immemorial and has also divided the heavens into twelve signs of the zodiac. Formerly, before the introduction of the decimal system, 12 and five times 12, the number 60, were used as the basis of the arithmetical system. The number 60 is divisible by 12 numbers, thus by one fifth of its own value, which is also a very high proportion! – We often find the number 12 in the Bible. The twelve tribes of Israel, the twelve disciples and the twelve baskets with the fragments of the two fishes and the five loaves with which Christ fed the five thousand, are only some instances. Tarot card 12 carries the numerical value 30, the number of the Holy Trinity linked with 0. We shall discuss the number further when dealing with tarot card 21 which is the inversion of the number 12 and which also has 3 as the sum of its digits.

In addition, this card carries the letter LAMED corresponding to the human arm, and thus is closely related to everything that lifts and unfolds itself like the arm. Prophetic revelations bring forth a divine expansion in man, out of which arises the idea of the revealed law.

DEATH

Numerical Value: 40

Letter: מ MEM

In this picture we see a skeleton holding a scythe, the ancient symbol of death. His posture and the position of the scythe in his hand imitate the shape of the letter MEM. The skeleton does not hold the scythe in the normal position for mowing. He holds it the wrong way round so that he cuts from left to right instead of from right to left. This shows that the skeleton has carried over to this level and retained the HANGED MAN's inverted attitude. All his thoughts and actions are diametrically opposed to those of ordinary men. In addition, however, he expresses with this inverted position of the scythe that there is also inverted death, that with this death there comes not *death*, but *life*. This is indicated by the red colour of the scythe and the blue of its blade. The skeleton mows down the person with the fire of the spirit and the faith of the soul.

This skeleton is nothing other than man's spirit. When the spirit embodied itself in matter and was born as a human being, it was forced *to die into* matter. It could no longer manifest its spiritual qualities, it could no longer *be* its own spiritual LIFE. It had to bear the qualities of the body and could manifest itself only to a very limited extent through the mortal frame.

DEATH

The spiritual consciousness was repressed and man became a mixture of a great many material and very few spiritual qualities. Thus he perceived the inner effect of his own spirit from the unconscious as the inner voice of an unknown, external being. The spirit struggled in man in order to be able to manifest itself through the body. The qualities of the body and those of the spirit are opposed to one another. The essential characteristics of the body are sloth and indolence; those of the spirit are fire and activity. From birth the spirit fights against the tyranny of the body. Starting with the most trivial matters right to the greatest human problems, man suffers from this conflict between body and spirit. For instance, the body would like to adopt a bad, lazy posture, because it is sluggish and weighed down by itself. The spirit seeks to triumph over the body in man and compels it to manifest spiritual powers. Every sport is a triumph over the body, in every movement the spirit seeks to manifest itself over the inertia of the body. This struggle begins already the moment we awake. The body would like to stay in bed and continue to sleep. But the spirit compels it, in spite of yawning, to rise, get dressed and go to work or pursue a sport. And so it goes on all day long. Even when faced with great problems, we act as Paul so aptly says in the Bible: '. . . for what I would, that do I not; but what I hate, that do I'. (Romans 7:15) *Who* is the *one* who wants something, and *who* is the one who nevertheless does *not* do it? And *who* is *the one* who does *not* want a thing and who is the one *who does it nevertheless?*

The spirit and the body are opposed and engaged in conflict; man constantly suffers from this inner struggle. Yet precisely this continuous suffering wakens his spiritual consciousness and compels him to find the way to his own spirit. One day he awakes and realises that he is not the body, the person, but his own higher Self, his own spirit, which should use the body as an instrument of manifestation, on no account, however, as an end in itself. This initial awakening is represented by tarot card 1. Here, for the first time, man has tasted spiritual freedom. Before experiencing this first spiritual level of consciousness, he was merely a blind slave dictated to by his instincts. Then his spiritual awareness increased step by step; gradually he lost the feeling that his own Self was an alien being outside himself, yet so uncannily well acquainted with him that it could speak to him through his conscience. He became aware that this 'being' above his personal consciousness was his own Self, his own spirit, WAS HE HIMSELF! – An ever greater light began to radiate in him, he experienced various states within himself until, at his present level of consciousness symbolised by tarot card 13, he grows conscious in his own Self, in his own spirit. According to a law of Nature formulated by Pythagoras, 'two things cannot be in the same place at once'. The spirit and the physical being, the person, cannot therefore simultaneously use the body of one person as an instrument of manifestation; one of them must disappear, be destroyed.

Since the person never possessed an actual individual existence, but merely borrowed its life from the spirit, the person must now disappear. Man, who has grown aware in the spirit, will henceforth without interference from the person, *consciously* be himself. His spiritual consciousness mows down the person, *kills it*. From now on the physical-vegetative powers will serve the body, but they will not take possession of its spiritual consciousness. In his consciousness the spirit will be master. The man who until now was a mixture of spirit and person becomes completely spiritual, completely *impersonal*. The spirit is the exact reverse, the opposite of the personal. The person stands for isolation and egoism; the spirit, however, destroys isolation, draws man into unity and makes him selfless.

The death of the person was already prepared at the previous levels. Man awakened, learned the meaning of justice, withdrew from the earthly world and gained control of his destiny, his karma. He experienced the titanic power of the spirit, true LOVE, and gladly accepted its domination. In addition, he had to learn to be objective and to be able to place himself in the position of his opponent. Through this he saw everything 'the wrong way round' like the 'hanged man'.

What has remained of his person? – Nothing, nothing whatever! Yet does this mean that man has grown indifferent, apathetic, inactive, listless and lifeless? – By no means! – On the contrary. Since he no longer has any personal problems, he has also no personal troubles, no personal sorrows. He is always at peace, yet he feels with twice his former empathy for the joys and sorrows of men, animals and plants. He does not interfere in things, but allows them to happen as God decrees, because he knows that nothing can happen without the will of God and everything that happens is for the best. We must learn from everything in order to come one step nearer to God on the long path. Without the will of God nothing could happen.

In the picture we see that only the body, the person, has disappeared: the two heads, the consciousness – the crown denotes spiritual consciousness, the hands and feet signify activity – are still there, they are fully alive. These hands swear that they live and that the feet continue to carry man on his way.

The two heads denote that even after becoming impersonal, man remains a man or a woman: he still belongs to a sex. The male head wears a crown. This means that the positive principle, the spirit, governs in man and that he is conscious in his spirit. Thus he is fully alive in his consciousness. His activity,· his consciousness, lives, only the person with its physical desires has been destroyed. There is an old saying which is a wonderful comment on this:

> Long did I resist,
> Finally I gave way
> When the old person turns to dust
> The new one greets the day.

And Goethe who was familiar with alchemistic transformation says:

And while this you cannot say:
Die and rise again!
You are but a shadow grey
On earth's darkling plain.

Tarot card 13 carries the numerical value 40 and the letter
MEM.

The numerical value 40 results from the number 13 and the
0, symbol of the universe. Unlike the previous number 12,
which was divisible by six numbers, the number 13 cannot be
divided at all. Therefore the number 13 is divisible only by 1,
GOD, and by 13, by itself; it is a prime number.

Everybody knows that the number 13 is an unlucky number,
but very few know why this is so. Those who know the tarot
cards regard 13 as an unlucky number because the card 13
stands for death. Yet it was not mere chance that the great
initiates, who created the tarot cards, made death identical
with the number 13 and the letter MEM. They chose these to
represent death because, as we shall see, they contain the ideas
of 'disappearance' and 'death'. For just as every circle contains *seven* smaller circles, whose diameter is one third of that
of the large circle, so every sphere, which is the three-dimensional projection of the circle in space, contains *thirteen*
smaller spheres, whose diameter is also exactly one third of the
diameter of the large sphere. Once we know that, we also
realize that the thirteenth sphere in the centre has 'disappeared',
it is invisible to the eyes of the external world: it is buried under
the twelve spheres surrounding it, thus it is 'dead'. That is
why the number 13 on the thirteenth tarot card means 'death'.
And because people lack a rational understanding of these
inner mathematical laws, yet deep down instinctively feel their
existence, they fear that the *thirteenth* person must die, if that
number is seated at table. But only the thirteenth! Not just
any one of them, not the first, nor the sixth or eighth, no – it is
the thirteenth who dies. Because twelve remain visible, therefore alive, the thirteenth has to become invisible, therefore
die, just as with the spheres the thirteenth one in the centre

disappears. It is quite remarkable that fate seems to know this law. For where a great religious or political leader is surrounded by twelve disciples, twelve generals or ministers, its validity can be observed. History provides examples enough in Jesus Christ, Julius Caesar, Napoleon and others.

The number 40 is also an allusion to the death of the spirit in matter. In symbolism, the cross and the square invariably stand for matter. As already explained in connection with tarot card 4, the first form of manifestation of creative power on entering the realm of dimensions, is the square and the cube, which is composed of six squares. All other crystal forms emerge from this first original form. The letter MEM is the second mother in the Greek alphabet. MEM lures the spirit into matter and through birth as a human being embodies it in matter. Birth into matter signifies death for the spirit, albeit an apparent death, as we already know. The spirit will rise again like Christ when it has attained self-awareness in matter. Or in other words, if and when man becomes self-conscious in the spirit. Thus man will rise again in his consciousness when he ceases to identify himself with his mortal body, in the knowledge that he used it only as an instrument of manifestation, and is not and never will be himself the body. The Christ figures of mediaeval painters swear to this fact and truth. They are depicted just as they emerge from the coffin holding a small flag of victory and resurrection and raising their right hand to swear: *For the spirit, for the Self, which we call* I, *there is no death, only eternal life!*

MEM also designates all rebirths arising from previous destruction. MEM symbolises all transformations, therefore the birth from the spiritual world into the body; and in death, the birth from the body into the spiritual world. The letter MEM, the MOTHER, was therefore for all men, for each one of us, the door through which we entered from the other world into this world, into the world of matter. We had to die into matter in order to be consciously reborn in the spirit, in order to learn that *our life is eternal.*

Tarot card 13 denotes the death of the little apparent ego, of the person, and the victory of the spirit. Therefore the same card is both end and beginning. Here, as in the case of tarot card 7, one period of development has ended and a new phase is embarked upon.

Tarot Card 14

BALANCE

Numerical Value: 50

Letter: ﬤ Nun

The French title of this tarot card is wrong. The card shows
us a level of development expressed much more adequately by
the word BALANCE. The woman on the card weighs something,
she *measures out* something, and in so doing is by no means
'temperate'. Our title is therefore: BALANCE.

Here again we see our queen of heaven, now, however,
without her crown. Instead, her hair is held in place by a golden
disk on her forehead. This shows her superior consciousness
linking her to the divine world. She wears the same red dress
as on tarot card 3. The azure blue robe which she wore as the
queen of heaven has become an outer garment, worn open at
the front to reveal the red dress. Both these garments have
yellow edging: there are even yellow stripes and a yellow
belt on the blue dress and a green lining is visible in the
neck. We already know that the red dress denotes her high
spirituality, the blue garment her staunch faith in God, the
yellow edging her intelligence, and the green lining her goodwill and humanity. Now she again wears the two large
wings which she had discarded in her roles as JUSTICE and
LOVE. She is released from earthly problems, she can once
more fly and soar up to heaven. She stands on the ground

only with the soles of her feet; to show this, her shoes are brown.

Beside her is the flower which has grown out of the ground and which we saw already on the pictures of the magician and the king. It is half-open and seems as if it expected to receive the water of life from the beautiful woman so that it can open fully.

The queen of heaven holds an urn in each hand. We recognise these as symbols of the two main currents of creation. The golden urn symbolises the positive-spiritual energies, the silver urn the negative-physical ones. The tension between the sources of the positive and negative poles is life itself. These energies bestow life on man and on everything that lives in creation. At the top of the head, under the crown, lies a brain centre in which the positive pole has its seat. The negative pole is situated in the coccyx at the base of the spine. The tension between the two poles in the spine constitutes our physical existence. Man, however, has the ability consciously to direct these two creative energies as he pleases. At certain points in his body he can accumulate positive or negative energies and elect to bring about changes in his body with these or to raise, wake and activate hitherto latent abilities from their state of dormancy. Ordinary men are ignorant of this and cannot direct these energies as they please. Those who know this secret, however, can be master of the creative energies and use or transform them at will.

In the picture we see the woman pouring the liquid from the silver urn into the golden one. This signifies that in this way she converts negative energies into positive ones. A chemical process takes place in the golden urn whereby everything it contains is turned into *positive spiritual* gold.

The woman considers carefully how much energy she can retain in the silver urn and how much she can pour into the golden urn without incurring danger. She gauges the energy. If she takes the correct amount, man makes rapid progress to his great goal. If, however, she measures inaccurately, his nerves crack under the strain.

This picture indicates that we can convert our physical energies into spiritual powers thereby wakening and making use of the previously inactive nerve centres in order to attain higher spiritual states. At tarot card 12 we were introduced to these seven spiritual centres. At this fourteenth level of consciousness man has come so far that he can and *may* wake and activate the latent physical nerve and brain centres where these spiritual centres, the chakras, are situated. He might have activated the chakras sooner, but that would have been dangerous. There are physical exercises designed to wake the chakras. Yet this procedure greatly endangers an immature man, for if his nerve and brain centres are not yet resilient enough, they will be deleteriously affected by the higher vibrations thus directed to them. On the other hand, the man who has already reached the higher level of consciousness and is capable of adequate resistance, may activate his chakras without incurring danger and sustain the inner tensions – so dangerous for those less developed than himself – as a normal condition.

We are not all alike and, according to our level of consciousness, we sustain various tensions in our nerves. If someone at a high level of development touches another person far below him, particularly if he lays his hand on that person's head, the latter will fall into a sleep-like trance. This, however, is not to be confused with hypnosis, for under hypnotic suggestion the subject loses his will-power. This contact does not destroy his consciousness and his will. On the contrary, his awareness and concentration are greatly increased. Yet the superior man must be able to control his powers to the extent that he can *administer them in the correct dose required.* If there is a very wide gap between the frequencies of his power currents and those of the man at the lower level, these *far higher* frequencies will cause serious nervous convulsions when directed into the nerves of the less mature man. There is one incident confirmed by many eyewitnesses, in which an apothecary in Dakshineswar (India) pestered the then already world-famous Indian saint, Rama Krishna, to transmit his high powers through contact. Eventually Rama Krishna gave in and, touching the man, sent his high frequencies into him. The apothecary went into such convulsions that he cried out loud and implored Rama Krishna to release him and restore his own normal state. Rama Krishna complied. We could also mention such cases in the West, but if we have understood these truths then further instances are superfluous. Man keeps progressing along the great path and, unknown to himself, his hitherto dormant energies unfold and become active. This inner procedure is greatly accelerated, however, if he *consciously* performs exercises involving no risk, which gradually increase the resilience of his nerves to the point where they can sustain higher tensions and their correspondingly higher frequencies.

At the level of the HANGED MAN these higher chakras have been recognised and consciously taken possession of. Tarot card 14 shows that man already knows the various sources of creative power and is not only familiar with the transition from the lower to the higher frequencies, but can also use and transform them. At this level he is able to convert physical energies into spiritual ones and *to dose* the various powers as he pleases. That is why the woman in the picture pours from the silver urn, symbolising physical energy, into the golden urn, symbolising spiritual energy, where, by an *inner* chemical process, the physical energy is transformed into spiritual. This art was known to the Rosicrucians and the alchemists and was called the 'royal art'. They passed on this secret to their disciples. The crusading knights brought this secret art, suitable only for mature men, from Asia and handed it on to their close friends in Europe. Thus as time went on, more and more small groups or lodges were formed, of which many great and famous men became members. To mention only a few of the most illustrious: Voltaire, Frederick the Great, Joseph II, Wieland, Lessing, Goethe, Mozart, Albrecht Dürer and many, many more. These mystical secrets were excellently depicted by Goethe in his masterpiece, *Faust*, by Mozart in his famous opera, *The Magic Flute*, and by Albrecht Dürer in many of his paintings. They were familiar with this inner process and also with the method which hastens our progress on the great path to the goal. In Asia and Europe we find traces of this secret knowledge; the writings of the alchemists and the Rosicrucians are based on the mysteries of the Cabbala. There are so many striking similarities between the pictorial language of the Rosicrucians and that of the tarot cards that it is obvious the tarot cards depict the same truths as the secret pictures of the Rosicrucians and the alchemists. It is probable that they stem from the same source.

Tarot card 14 carries the numerical value 50, composed of the sum of the digits of the number 14 and 0, the symbol of boundless space. It also carries the letter NUN.

The number 14 contains the number 7 twice. In this instance, two times the number 7 means the twice reflected life which animates the material body and the spiritual being of man. The sum of the digits is the number 5 which was discussed in connection with tarot card 5. Now, however, the number 50, ten times 5, therefore a 5 with the 0, of which the sum of the digits is the number of Christ, 5, has a much deeper meaning. In discussing the number 5, we saw that the exterior pentagonal shape signified the human form. On this tarot card it implies the inner vital current, which likewise flows pentagonally in the body:

In Albrecht Dürer's painting of the Crucifixion an angel stands on either side of the crucified Christ. Each holds a goblet to catch the blood springing like a fountain from the hands of Christ on the Cross. The painting shows us the current of the creative principle, the Christ-current. After flowing through the whole human body, crucified in time and space, it is emitted from five points: from the two hands, the two feet and from the solar plexus – therefore from the five wounds of Christ. Dürer, who was himself an initiated Rosicrucian and familiar with the truth about the vital current and the mystery of physical energies converted into spiritual power, frequently depicted this truth in his paintings. These initiates were not allowed to speak about these things, but they could represent the truth in secret figures or paintings. Thus they wished to attract attention in their own way.

The letter NUN alludes to the name Immanuel, which in the Bible is the name of the divine child. Immanuel means: 'God in us', therefore the higher Self animating man, which said of itself: 'I AM THE LIFE!' – The name IMMANUEL therefore means the life in man. When man becomes conscious in *life itself*, he is resurrected in IMMANUEL, in Christ. NUN is the solar energy which endows us with life. NUN is the image of begotten and reflected being, therefore a fruit. The old person has died and the new one is already here as IMMANUEL, as the *divine child*, not yet grown-up.

THE DEVIL

Numerical Value: 60

Letter: ס SAMEKH

The principal figure in this picture is a gigantic devil. Just as the Devil is always depicted with a goat's head and hooved feet but with human hands, here, too, he is a mixture of man and goat. He has two mighty horns between which his hair extends to the top of his head, where the highest nerve centre, the Sahasrara chakra, seat of the positive pole, is located. This shows that the Devil has already activated and used this centre. He has a five-pointed star on his forehead!

The Devil or Satan carries the symbols of all four elements and of the two sexes. The red colour of his head symbolises the spirit and the element fire. The two beautiful plumed wings of the queen of heaven have become, on Satan's shoulders, two gigantic bat wings which he uses to fly through boundless space, thus establishing himself as ruler of the air. The upper part of his body and his arms are light in colour and therefore also symbolise the element air. The lower part of his body is covered with fish scales indicating the element water. His legs are brown and instead of feet he has the hooves of a goat. These symbolise the element earth. Satan is ruler of the four elements, known to present-day scholars as 'states of matter'. As the universe was formed from the four elements, Satan rules over the whole material world. After the Last Supper, Christ said: 'Rise, let us be going: behold, he is at hand that doth betray me.' (St Matthew 26: 46) His disciples knew that this was SATAN.

In this material world only Satan can be ruler, for he is the law of matter manifesting itself in contraction, cooling and solidification. As long as Satan remains the unconscious law of matter, he is a law of Nature and in his place. If, however, man makes the law of matter conscious in himself, identifying himself with it, it becomes a living spirit in him. This law which has come alive through the human spirit is Satan. In his spiritual aspect he is the exact opposite of the spirit, he is the antagonist, for the laws of the spirit and the laws of matter are the mirror images of each other. Satan as such has no kind of independent existence. He can only live in and become alive through man, for man alone can make a living spirit from the law of matter when he identifies his consciousness with this law. Thus it is man himself who bestows life on Satan. And yet, Satan, this spirit which has come alive only through man, can react by throwing back man's reflection, luring him into ruin, hell and perdition.

The magician's wand and the queen of heaven's sceptre have become a burning torch which Satan holds in his right hand. He rules over matter, therefore also over the human body; the flame of the torch is the fire, the heat of the body, set alight by the immanent spirit and animating the body. But the moment the fire of the spirit animates the body, the latter falls under the rule of the law of matter, therefore under the rule of Satan. And because Satan dominates the human body, he also dominates the fire which animates it and manifests itself in the two great human instincts, those of self-preservation and the preservation of the species.

In animals these two instincts operate without interference from the intellect, precisely because animals have no intellect and live entirely according to the laws and scheme of Nature. If an animal is prevented from keeping rigidly to this scheme,

it dies. For instance, if ants cannot feed on what Nature prescribes, they die. If they cannot couple at the exact time decreed
by Nature, they die a wretched death. They cannot postpone
their union should anything intervene. The higher an animal
ranks in the vast scale of Nature, the greater its adaptability,
yet this too has its limits. As a general rule animals have to
adhere strictly to the laws of Nature.

Without the intellect man too, would have to adhere to the
prescribed scheme of Nature in the same unconscious way as
animals. Man, however, possesses an excellent intellect which
helps him to attain consciousness. It has the function of a
mirror in which he recognises himself. The intellect also
enables him to disregard the laws of Nature and to adapt himself to changes in his environment. He can survive potential
disasters or unimaginable privations without any real harm,
even if he cannot eat and drink what Nature prescribes. His
sex life, too, may be subjected to the control of his intellect
and will-power. On the one hand this adaptability gives him
a very great advantage over animals, but at the same time it
involves the very great danger that, assisted by his intellect,
he strays from the path of Nature and destroys his healthy
instincts. His essentially healthy natural needs may be per-
verted into ends in themselves and thus cause physical and
mental disorders. He may even become addicted and thus sell
and enslave his soul to the Devil. In this way man delivers
himself into Satan's power, into the power of the Serpent on
the tree of knowledge of good and evil. . . .

We see that the symbol of reason and intellect, the symbol
of Mercurial power, figures in this picture as Satan's sexual
organ. This means that Satan controls man through his reason,
penetrates him through his consciousness and in this way
brings him under his influence. Without the human intellect
Satan could not be 'Satan'. Without man he would remain an
unconscious law of Nature.

In his left hand Satan holds the sexual organs in their coital
position; the positive-male and the negative-female one. His

right arm bears the inscription SOLVE, which means SEVER. On his left arm is inscribed COAGULA, which means UNITE. – What does he sever and what does he unite? What the Vedanta philosophy already asserted thousands of years ago has now also been established by science, namely, that in the very beginnings of time both sexes were present together in the human body. Man was a bisexual being; he was androgynous like an angel. This notion of angels as androgynous beings has been handed down to us by every religious tradition – whether in Europe or in Asia, among the Indians of America or the Negroes of Africa. Perhaps these traditions, unanimous on this point, represent the truth, although that truth is somewhat less simple than the religions imply. Bisexual creatures have nothing to do with hermaphrodites – the name is composed of Hermes and Aphrodite – who are *neither* man *nor* woman. The androgynous being is man and woman in one person. The Bible, too, which gives us one of the oldest stories of the creation and development of mankind, asserts that man was once bisexual. For in the beginning, Adam, who personifies the primitive form of man in one being, carried the two sexes within himself, and Eve appears only when God takes her out of Adam's body. We read in the Bible how God caused a deep sleep to fall upon Adam, took one of his ribs and from it made Woman, Eve. Thus the Bible describes the same development as science affirms today, although in scientific terms it did not happen so simply and quickly but may have taken millions of years. Satan, the law of matter, separated the two sexes so that progeny can be begotten and born, and made of each sex an independent being. He therefore SEVERED the two sexes – SOLVE! But then he reunited them in an outwardly experienced sexual act – COAGULA. During this, however, the sexes are together for only a brief period. After physical union they must fall apart and once again continue their physical existence independently, separated from the other half. In various religions and in science the theory is advanced that the two beings, which were once only *one* bisexual being and were

separated by the dislocation of the sexes, are still seeking each
other even now in their earthly existence. They still have a
sense of belonging and yearn to become one again, to have *a
single* EGO. Beethoven, the titanic genius, writes to his un-
attainable mistress, Therese Brunswick: 'Oh, thou my angel,
my all, my "I" . . .'

Thus, as we see in the picture, Satan, the law of matter, has
separated men into the sexes and brought them together again
in outward physical union. That is why he holds the sexual
organs in coital position in his left hand. But the union is only
physical.

In the picture we also see the sexes personified as two
figures, half-man, half-devil: a small male devil and a small
female one. They are tied by heavy rope to the pedestal on
which the Devil stands. They are separated from each other –
indeed, severed, as the inscription says – SOLVE – but at the
same time they are also eternally chained together through
their *inner identity in the spirit* which manifests itself as physical-sexual desire and physical-sexual energy. The inscription
on the left arm says as much: COAGULA – unite. Thus they
cannot live with each other, nor can they live without each
other. Yet this has not come about so swiftly that man perceives it clearly and is aware of it. It has been prepared over a
long period, particularly at the level of consciousness of tarot
card 6, where he had to choose between the right and the wrong
path. The development continued at the ninth level where he
already withdrew from worldly life and like a hermit acquainted
himself with the inner world and the inner life. In addition, he
experienced true love, selflessness, at the eleventh level.

At the twelfth level he learned to see things in a way which
ordinary men would call 'upside down'. He further experienced
mystical death and learned to convert negative energies into
positive ones. The inevitable consequence now was to be
able to transform sexual energy into creative power. In his
soul he was ready for this. With the experience of mystical
death, memories of his entire life sprang to mind. And he had

to admit that sexual energy had really deceived him. He had expected to find happiness in physical union but had never found it. For physical gratification was still a long way off from happiness and the expected fulfilment. At the very moment when he thought he was about to attain perfect fulfilment in physical union, the whole tension blazed up like a firework but was at the same time already burned out and extinguished. He could never arrest the ecstasy, never hold on to it as an enduring happiness. There remained only an insatiable longing for the happiness he had never found.

And what remains for him when he is old and no longer able to experience physical love? Again, nothing, nothing whatever! And he went on to ask himself what it was that he was trying to achieve in sexual union, since he had not been truly gratified by what it had offered him. – That was it! All his life he had searched for a human being who was his other half, his complement. Love is the manifestation of a power which forces two complementary halves to reunite. The unconscious drive to unite is in fact called 'love'. Man seeks fulfilment of this urge and believes it possible in physical union. Yet he has to concede that he has never found what he was seeking. He sought a real, *lasting* unity! He wanted a unity in which he was identical with the loved one, he wanted to become identical with the EGO of his partner. He wanted to destroy the I-YOU relationship so that he and the loved one could be *one single* EGO. And this is not possible. – Why? – Because *the body* stands in the way. Indeed! The law of matter, SATAN, intervenes. The resistance of matter, of the body, does not allow two beings who love each other to become ONE in external, material reality. Man has had to recognise a paradox, an impossibility and a discrepancy: that he wants to experience inner unity with his partner *in the body*, and that it is *the body itself which resists and prevents this oneness.*

Why then does he seek this physical union? Why has he longed for it since childhood, since the initial wakening of consciousness? He knew that only complete unity and not merely *physical manifestation* could gratify him and give him true happiness. And if this is not possible in the body, he does not want it at all. Yet unity must be possible otherwise he could not desire it! It can be achieved only in a certain state in which he is not prevented by the body. Man was once in this state, he is keenly aware of this and longs to recapture it. Somewhere and at some time he was in it, but he has fallen out. This was *the fall from Paradise*! But he must return there! He must! He has fallen *out of* this state precisely because he was born *into* the body. And if that is so, he intends to renounce the substitute, physical union, which is incomplete and can never gratify him. Compromises will not do any more. He has to realise that the body cannot wish for this true union, having itself prevented him from attaining and experiencing it. In the spirit, however, it is possible to experience and realise the urge for unity, true love, and in this way man will find release from bondage.

He did not succeed in coming so far all at once. But at the level of consciousness represented by tarot card 15, he frees himself from this enslavement. He transforms the energy tying him to the opposite sex into its primitive form and uses it in its converted, or properly speaking, re-converted form as creative power, as spiritual power of the creative principle, Logos.

And now let us return to the star of Christ on Satan's forehead. If we know that sexual energy is the manifestation of creative power in matter, in the body, then we understand how Satan is involved with it. The same power which as sexual energy chains the two figures together at Satan's pedestal, in the chakras of the lowest nerve centres, is manifested as creative power, as the power of Christ's spirit, in the higher brain centres situated in the head. If we are able to sublimate, if we can re-convert sexual energy into creative power, then we have conquered Satan with his own power. For we can only complete this transformation with the help of the laws of

Nature, with the help of Satan. Then man is set free from the satanic chains.

> From the power that holds all in fee
> He who overcomes himself is free!

say Goethe. When man experiences tarot card 15 within himself, he reaches this level; he is no longer a creature of instincts, a sexual being. Even if he found the other half of his celestial being, from which Satan had severed him, in an *earthly* form, he would still consciously experience a transcendingly blissful *spiritual* union with this complementary half. For unconsciously he always carried his complementary half in the depths of his soul. The animus and the anima are one *in the spirit*!

The Devil in the picture carries both sexes within himself. *He* does *not* need to sever them from each other within himself. He has a red beard, therefore in his head, in the spirit, he is masculine-positive. His breasts are fully developed like those of a nursing mother, therefore feminine-negative. His sexual organ is again male, no longer in the physical, but in the spiritual sense. His sexual organ is the human intellect, his intelligence with which he penetrates man, takes possession of him and enslaves him. At the level of consciousness of tarot card 15 man has liberated himself from this possession.

Tarot card 15 carries the numerical value 60, which consists of the sum of the digits of the number 15, therefore of 6, and the o symbolising boundless space. It carries the letter SAMEKH.

The number 5 is less by half than the number of creation, 10, and the number 15 is greater by half than the number of creation, 10. The number 15 is therefore divisible by the divine number 3 and by the number of Christ, 5. The result of the multiplication of these two numbers is 15. The sum of the digits of the number 15 is 6, and if we add o, we obtain the number 60, the numerical value of this card. The number 60 is divisible by 12 numbers, therefore by the *fifth* part. There is no number which has more related numbers: 1, 2, 3, 4, 5, 6,

10, 12, 15, 20, 30, 60. It is no mere chance that Satan should carry this number. He has to have a great number of connections! – It is worth while reflecting on this number a little. This will increase our understanding of many things.

The letter SAMEKH represents a weapon. At this level of consciousness man has to conquer this weapon and gain possession of it in order to defend and protect himself against any influence from outside or inside. The spherical shape of this letter is reminiscent of an arch. The closed circle is, however, also the well-known symbol of the serpent biting its own tail. SAMEKH also means 'antipole' (of the sexes) and 'Nahash' the dragon guarding the threshold.

THE LIGHTNING-STRUCK TOWER

Numerical Value: 70

Letter: ע AYIN

In this picture we see a strongly built tower which has been struck by lightning – not originating from a thunder-cloud, but from the sun. The lightning strikes deep into the thick fabric of the tower which is ripped into two parts, the upper part tumbling to the ground. The tower is red, the colour symbolising spirituality; at the top it has green and yellow stripes signifying love of humanity and intelligence. The tower has four crenels. The number four stands for matter. This reveals that the tower symbol has to do with the material aspect of man.

The tower has one door and three windows. Two of them are on the same level, the third one is placed above the other two so that all three form a triangle. The door symbolises the human solar plexus. This is where we were tied to the body at conception by a magic cord and this is where we shall again leave the body at death. The two windows next to each other are our two eyes through which we look out of our material body and link ourselves with the outside world. The upper window is the 'third eye', a nerve centre in which the spiritual centre known in the Vedanta philosophy as the 'Ajna chakra' has its seat. Through this centre man is connected to the spiritual world; through this centre he achieves vision.

From the tower heavy bricks fall down on two figures who have themselves fallen from it. Curiously, however, the bricks hit only the man who is not wearing a crown and he falls to the ground lifeless. The other man has kept his crown on his head even during the fall. He is not hit by bricks. They fall beside him and he escapes uninjured and alive.

The two figures have multi-coloured clothing. The dead man wears a red tunic. He has a blue sleeve on his left arm. The man with the crown wears a blue tunic but his right arm has a red sleeve and his left leg a yellow stocking. The colours of the costumes show that it is of no intrinsic avail for a man to be spiritual; if he is not *aware* of it, he must die when the tower collapses. The other man has endured his destiny with complete faith in God; but because he was fully conscious in undergoing all his trials – the crown denotes consciousness – he has survived the fall and remained perfectly unharmed.

In the picture we also see sixteen coloured balls which represent the number 16, the number of this tarot card.

This picture shows an event which inevitably occurs once in the life of every man who proceeds on the path to the great goal.

The previous levels of consciousness have been experienced in his inner world. Outside, in the external world, neither his friends nor his closest relatives have noticed anything of this. Now, however, something happens to him which has a profound effect on his outer destiny and calls into question his entire external life. How this happens varies from one person to another and depends upon his surroundings, in what family and in which country he lives and works. In countries which are subjected to the ravages of war, many people experience the total collapse of everything around them. They lose their means of livelihood, and their whole family may be uprooted and scattered across the world. They lose their material possessions and their friends. They are ruined. They have to stand entirely on their own two feet and turn only to themselves for help, for nothing else is left. They have to build a whole new life. In past and present wars millions of people have experienced what is symbolised by this card. The unconscious ones have fallen spiritually and can never again rise, recover and proceed, even if their bodies survive. As human beings they are destroyed like the dead man in the picture.

Yet some people who have come so far that they are not the 'person', not the unconscious slave of their instincts, but are conscious in their Self, in their spirit – those who are able to keep the crown on their heads – they will be able to build an entirely new life. Such people have lost nothing, but rather gained.

Even if a person has not experienced a war in his external life, the moment comes once – for those who consciously continue along the great path this is certainly true – in which something happens to threaten his faith, to rob him of his inner security, and to destroy him. Then he has to make every effort to concentrate all his inner powers so that he does not fall, so that he stays on his feet. This can take many forms. It can happen that someone loses the being most dearly beloved by him, the one with whom he had grown together in the soul. But the spiritually conscious man knows that there is no death, only eternal life, and that he must only have the patience to wait until time has run out on the cosmic clock and the hour strikes for him, too, to follow the loved one. Until that time he has not lost this beloved being, for he always retains his spiritual bond. Thus he does not collapse but stays on his feet.

Others may go through this trial in the context of their work, no matter whether their job puts them in a leading position or not. It may be that they are attacked, that their honesty is doubted or that they must innocently suffer reproaches and accusations and cannot even defend themselves against time.

Some are made the butts of ridicule through their ill-bred children, others again through an unworthy father or mother, and a slur is cast on their good name. The potential circumstances through which men can be shaken to the foundations of their existence are so many that they cannot all be enumerated. Fate exploits the personal situation and possibilities of each individual wherever and whenever he can be hit hardest and destroyed. But those who have already experienced mystical death, who, like the sphinx, are superior to their destiny and are able to regard it as if it were someone else's fate, who know that one can harm only the body but never the spirit, those people cannot be destroyed. Such a person knows that whatever men think about him or however they may treat him does not really affect either his stature, his honesty or his personal attractions. He is as he is and no opinion of his fellow-men will change him. He knows that God is in him and that this trial also has been sent by God – *hence the lightning from the sun!* – in order that he may learn something important from it. And when he has passed the test God will help him out of the destruction and enable him to build a new life and to free himself of all evils. We know of many great affairs, past and present, in which innocent men have been attacked, accused, condemned, imprisoned, deported and even executed. Yet the conscious, superior man could never be destroyed in his being, not even on the gallows.

When Alexander the Great was in India with his army, he met a famous Yogi. He spoke to him and liked him very much. He wanted the Yogi to accompany him to Macedonia. The Yogi, however, did not want to go. Whereupon Alexander said to him: 'If you do not come with me, I will have you put to death.' At this the Yogi laughed and answered: 'You want to kill *me*? – *Me*? – You cannot even see me. You can only have my body put to death, but never my EGO which dwells in my body and which I AM.' And Alexander was so impressed by this reply that he bestowed generous gifts on him and continued on his way in a very thoughtful frame of mind. Thus the incident has been handed down to us. The man at this level of consciousness must behave in exactly the same way: he must have the same attitude as the great Yogi had towards Alexander. With inner security he must endure fate and always know that ignorant men can only torture and harm his apparent ego, his person, but never his spiritual, true EGO, never his higher SELF. And when all his troubles are over, his values will not have left him but will again come to light in the external world. He will be able to resume his proper role in life.

If a man is able to keep his crown on his head, then he will always remain a king, ruler over his destiny. Yet he had to experience this test, he had to go through this destruction in order to learn not to put the trivial before the important, the inessential before the essential. 'For what shall it profit a man, if he shall gain the whole world, and lose his own soul?' (Mark 8 : 36), Christ says to us. As long as we do not lose our soul, we can lose everything else and still have EVERYTHING.

This destruction in the external world is caused, even if quite unconsciously, by unconscious men who do not wear the crown. In particular the people who are especially prone to this are those who prophesy and anticipate only evil for others and for themselves, or again those who are constantly afraid without admitting it. Such people tend to bring down this destruction on themselves by directing their own fates towards such a calamity with many minor or major actions. Unconsciously they feel that they can only be liberated from their constant fear and misconceptions by actual experience of the evil they are perpetually afraid of. Afterwards they see that they have had no reason at all to be afraid – usually they do not even know the object of their fear. The greatest evil of our time is fear. People are afraid of war; they are afraid of foreigners, therefore they wage wars. They are afraid of poverty, they are afraid of losing their marriage partner, a child or a loved one. They are afraid of illness, accidents and of universal devastation by the atomic bomb – and finally, there are a great number who *are afraid of fear itself*!

There are, however, a few who are not afraid, who are convinced that there exists a higher power than the power of men and that this power always gives us what *is best* for us. Therefore if ruin were to strike, both in man and in the external world it could destroy *only the illusory values*, but never the true, real ones. For this reason these happy few do not require the experience of destruction which is needed by those who are full of fear.

They do not seek or cause destruction, consciously or unconsciously. And if they have to experience it externally they do not feel destroyed. They already know that life itself can never be destroyed and annihilated. Life survives everything. Not even matter can be destroyed, for when a house has been flattened by a bomb or a natural disaster, the materials of which it was built still lie scattered where the house used to stand and only the shape which was built from these materials has been transformed into raw, shapeless matter. The material world also derives its life from LIFE. Destruction only causes matter to become shapeless and the LIFE which has freed itself from this matter to return to the great universal, eternal LIFE, to GOD.

Those who have experienced the total destruction symbolised by tarot card 16 command unshakeable, absolute security, absolute trust in themselves, in eternal life, in GOD.

Tarot card 16 carries the numerical value 70 which consists of the sum of the digits of the number 16 and the 0, symbol of boundless space. It also carries the letter AYIN.

The number 16 consists of four times four which expresses that matter rebels against matter. Four is the number of matter. If, however, we take four times four, we get ultra-materialised matter which already means destruction. Ultra-matter is hate, ruin and destruction.

The sum of the digits of the number 16 is 7, thus again the key number of the material level, of the three-dimensional world. Together with the 0 we obtain seven times the number of perfect creation, thus $7 \times 10 = 70$. This implies the promise that from the ruins a new and higher life will arise.

The letter AYIN corresponds to the name Hazad, which may be translated as the 'strong one' and the 'brave one'. The strong and brave and conscious cannot be destroyed by anything. This card means that the Holy Spirit acts like a god of matter: 'divine destruction' which invariably leads to life. In Hindu mythology this corresponds to the god Shiva, god of destruction and renewal of life through destruction.

THE STARS

Numerical Value: 80

Letter: **פ** PE

Again we see the queen of heaven, but now without any attributes: no crown on her head, no wings on her shoulders, no golden chain at her neck, no sceptre in her hand, no clothes on her body and no shoes on her lovely feet. Her hair falls loosely in natural curls which cover her shoulders and back. She is as naked as the day she was born.

She is in a fair meadow amidst a beautiful landscape. She kneels on her left knee, her right foot before her on the grass.

She has the same two urns which she held for the transformation of energies in her role as personified BALANCE. Then she had poured the waters of life from one urn into the other. Now she pours the positive energy, symbolised by water, from the golden urn in her right hand into a river. From the silver urn in her left hand, she pours the negative energy first onto firm ground – onto the earth – to soften it up, from where it too flows into the river which carries it to all living creatures that they may drink of it. This water is the water of universal love, the water of life.

To her right we again see the flower which has appeared in these pictures; first in that of the magician, where it was still a closed bud, then with the queen of heaven, where it was half-open, and finally in the picture of 'Balance', where it waited for the water of life in order to open fully. Now it has opened and is in full bloom. It reveals its innermost being, all its treasures, it hides nothing. A blue butterfly perches in the cup of the flower and drinks its nectar. In the sky which forms the background we see eight stars of various sizes. The smallest blue star is above the woman's head. Four medium-sized yellow stars form a square. Two larger blue stars are placed opposite each other. All these stars have eight sharp points. The eighth star, however, actually incorporates two eight-pointed stars. The larger star on top is yellow, the smaller one behind it is green.

If we have attentively followed the explanations of the cards, we will have guessed that this beautiful naked woman symbolises the soul of man. After the terrible collapse of his personality he has discarded the last superficial disguises and masks. Nothing has remained of him except what he is in absolute reality, HE HIMSELF. Naked, completely unveiled, just as God has created his soul, a living spirit in his true higher Self. He no longer possesses anything, for what he possesses as an earthly human being does not belong to him, he merely uses it. Even if he does not yet possess the two currents of life he can control and direct them. He pours the positive and the negative currents from the golden and silver urns into the great river of life, from which all men may then drink. He does not need to retain any for himself; no longer does he pour the two currents from one urn into the other for himself, as on tarot card 14 in his role as 'Balance', rather, he passes on to his fellow-men all the treasures and the truth about the waters of life which he has found in the course of his long journey along the path, so that with the help of these secrets they may progress more swiftly. Where it is necessary he gives positive-masculine energies; he encourages the faint-hearted and helps them to make headway in the struggle of life and to soldier on to victory. Where it is necessary he gives negative-feminine energies: he gives tenderness and comfort, under-

standing and love. His urns are inexhaustible. The more
courage and power, the more understanding and love he gives,
the more powerfully and abundantly these pour from the source
of his 'urns' – from his heart.

The flower of his soul, his consciousness, has opened. He
has made everything conscious within himself, he has nothing
left in his unconscious, that is to say, *he no longer has an unconscious*. He has acquired self-knowledge and he manifests all
the treasures which God has given him and which he has found
himself. The higher beings of creation descend from the higher
worlds and settle in his open soul, just as the butterflies flutter
all the way down from the sky to the open flower and drink
nectar from its cup. The butterfly therefore denotes a close
inner link with the higher worlds. Just as the angels of God
descended to Jacob at the well in the desert, so man when he
has reached this high state communicates in his innermost
Self with the beings of the higher worlds, with the spirits of
God. Though he be ever so alone among ordinary men and
feel like Jacob in the desert, he is nevertheless like Jacob at the
fountain of the life-source. He drinks from it and never feels
alone. GOD is always with him.

At this level of consciousness man has no other thought, no
other desire than to participate in the great work, in the redemption of the world. For him this is no sacrifice, no denial, for it
gives him great pleasure to see that even those who were
previously groping their way in the darkness are following him
and making progress. It gives him pleasure and satisfaction to
learn that his followers already recognise what is essential in
life and do not subordinate it to the inessential. It pleases him
to see that people follow his guidance and, free of anxiety, with
deep faith, merge into the great whole like tiny molecules,
become children of God and thus, as Christ said, the salt of the
earth.

A human being at the level symbolised by tarot card 17 is
like a shining star in the dark sky. Just as the planets shine in
the night because they reflect the light of the sun, so man

passes on the light he receives from God. He radiates love and light to all who come into contact with him and he shines like a star with his wisdom and deep faith in God. In the picture we see four yellow stars in the shape of a square. The square invariably symbolises matter. Man therefore radiates his wisdom into the world of matter. He teaches his fellow-men about the profound mysteries of Creation and of human nature. He explains rationally the laws of life and destiny; he wants to speak to men through the intellect.

Above the woman's head we see a small blue star. It shows her personal light, her devout faith. She can never have low, common thoughts nor concern herself with common or obscene things. Her person has been purified, it radiates purity. The two larger stars just above the small blue one symbolise by their beautiful colour the higher mental powers, which represent purity and devotion to God. The much larger double star consists of a yellow and a green star. The yellow star is larger than the green one behind it. This star symbolises the higher Self, man's spirit which manifests itself through wisdom and high intelligence as well as through devotion to God. The spirit shines like a bright star through his person, through his soul, and spreads light around him wherever he may be. Just as the Star of Bethlehem showed the three Magi the way to the birthplace of the Redeemer, so man shines and radiates at this level and shows each living creature the way to redemption.

Tarot card 17 carries the numerical value 80 which is composed of the sum of the digits of the number 17 and the 0, symbol of boundless space. It carries the letter PE.

The number 17 is divisible only by the number 1 and by itself. It is therefore a prime number, invariably denoting isolation. It is a reference to the fact that at this level man isolates himself increasingly from the world. Objective, spiritual, he is open to everyone; he freely reveals his perceptions. But he maintains silence about his personal affairs; he does not even find these of interest to himself, far less wanting to burden other people with them. The numerical value 80 shows that he is already connected to the 'infinite', the horizontal eight, and is linked with the 0 – 80 is divisible by 8 numbers – and that he has an *inner* relationship with a great many people. Thus he is isolated only in the person – like the number 17 – yet he has an inner, spiritual relationship to human beings, numerical value 80. The mouths of the two urns placed together result in the symbol of infinity, the horizontal 8, thus ∞. This we have already seen on the magician's head on tarot card 1 and on the head of 'Love' on tarot card 11, and on tarot card 8 as the two scales.

In hieroglyphics the letter PE means 'language'. It is therefore the continuation of the letter BETH on tarot card 2, which in hieroglyphics means the 'mouth'. Then the high priestess still had her mouth closed; she did not want to divulge the secrets of the other world and she kept silence. Now, on this card, language flows through the human mouth; the 'language' is that of the creative energies from the mouths of the two urns and it is handed on in this way. In this instance 'language' means the spreading of the cabbalistic 'fluid', of knowledge.

THE MOON

Numerical Value: 90

Letter: **צ** TZADDI

This tarot card is dominated by the large lunar disk containing the face of a beautiful woman in profile. Her face is kind, full; it puts one in mind of a good mother. The background of the disk is blue like the sky. The rear part of the head consists of a blue, a white and a yellow stripe. As we already know from the previous explanations, the blue background and blue stripe denote devotion and faith in God, the white stripe stands for purity, and the yellow one for shrewdness, intelligence, understanding. The lunar disk is set in eighteen long yellow points, which surround the moon like rays of light. The eighteen points refer to the number of this card. Between the long yellow points there are short red ones. The yellow points are the intellectual powers emanating from the intelligent head, and the red points in the background denote the spirituality manifested through the woman's intellectual powers. From the red points of light large coloured drops fall to the ground like leaves from a tree. There are yellow, green and red drops. This means that from this face, from this lunar being, goodwill and humanity as well as intelligence and spirituality radiate to all living creatures on earth.

Below, on the ground, we see a landscape divided into two

parts. We feel that there is a great difference, a sharp distinction between the foreground and the background. At the entrance to the background, to the right and left, we see two massive towers. They are reminiscent of the one struck by freak lightning on tarot card 16. Here the towers do not have four, but three square crenels. This already denotes a certain spiritualisation of matter. Both towers are built of heavy bricks and each has one window. On the left tower the window is open; on the right one it is closed.* At the foot of the right tower we see an open door leading to the foreground. The occupant of this tower has left – this explains the closed window – but he has not gone towards the horizon but rather to the foreground of the picture. He first had to withdraw into the blue pool. In the other tower there is no door, only an open window. These towers correspond to the two pillars of Solomon, 'Jachin' and 'Boaz', and to the two legs of Logos, one of which stands on the ocean, the other on the ground.

Between the towers a path from the right-hand side of the foreground leads into the distance. It is red and therefore a purely spiritual path!

In front of the towers are two animals. A white dog and a black wolf. We already know that the white dog symbolises something pure, the black wolf, on the other hand, something diabolic and material. The two animals look up at the moon and howl full-throatedly. They are the guardians of the threshold.

In the foreground there is a large, round, blue pool. In it we see many small tufts of water grass and a huge red crayfish. The pool symbolises the human memory in which rest all the things that have happened in our lives, and the crayfish is our spirit, our higher Self, which withdraws to the pool of memories to make the final settling of accounts. The path leading into the distance between the two towers passes this pool. We see how the path breaks up into fragments between the towers, becoming continuous again in the distance.

* Due to an error on the part of the artist, this is not properly illustrated in the picture.

We have a sense of a solemn, dramatic stillness in this picture. At this moment something decisive must happen to affect the entire future life of the man who experiences this level. After all the experiences of his previous states, he arrives at the great threshold where he *actually*, and not merely inwardly, leaves all earthly things behind and crosses over to the purely spiritual world as at the moment of death. He crosses the threshold between resurrection and life – and death. First, like the cray-fish in the depths of the pool, he withdraws to the depths of his being where all memories rest, to digest and ponder over what has happened to him in this life. He digests all that he has experienced and learned with his fellow-men, with his family and in his work, he takes stock of and clarifies everything. He digests his entire earthly life and comes to terms with it. When he has struggled through this stage of development, he will inwardly be as he was at the moment of birth and as he will be at the moment of death. He brought nothing with him, nor can he take anything away. When he entered this world he was simply *here*, in his consciousness he had neither parents nor friends, neither marriage partner nor children nor grand-children, he possessed nothing, he did not know what it means to possess. For him the universe was a connected whole, that simply existed and with which he had had no dealings as yet, and which had not yet fettered him. Now he has reached this state once more. Nothing belongs to him personally, but he himself does not belong to anybody either. He is free of all that has stood in the way of his freedom, just as we shall be free in death. He leaves everything behind and follows in the footsteps of the spiritual titans who have preceded him on this path to resurrection, to eternity. First, however, he must enter upon the path which leads out of earthly, illusory reality, from the pool of 'withdrawal into the Self' and of 'reflection on all that has happened', he must pass between the towers, if the guardians of the threshold let him cross at all, and continue on his way. As he proceeds he must be very careful to trace only the steps of his great predecessors who also once crossed this threshold. He must follow these titans faithfully. He must not miss his footing: a single false step and he falls back to where he started. He cannot afford to stumble at this stage, since it is already a matter of life and death.

The passage is narrow. The towers stand close together, thus forcing him to go through this narrow gap. And there are also the two animals, guardians of the threshold, who do not want to let him through. These animals, who sometimes resemble dragons and sometimes Cerberus of Greek mythology, can be seen at church entrances both in Europe and in Asia. Who are these guardians of the threshold? And why is one white and the other black? Why does the white dog at least not let him through, since his very colour shows that he symbolises something pure, spiritual and beautiful? Indeed! That is precisely the reason!

We recognise in these two animals the two strange creatures on tarot card 10, on the wheel of fortune. There the wolf was still a devil; but the dog was already a dog. They denote the instinct of preservation of the species and the instinct of self-preservation. There they still rotated in the destiny of man, even though he was already superior and impartial like the sphinx. Now, however, he will finally leave these two behind him, just as in death we leave our desires and instincts here on earth. Now the two animals have been divested of their attributes. The wolf, previously a devil, no longer has his Neptune's trident, nor the dog his Mercury's staff. They have therefore much less power over man. The wolf, who as the instinct of preservation of the species once exercised a 'diabolic' power over him, is now no more than an animal. The same is true of the dog, who once acted as mortal fear in the human consciousness. Neither of them can any longer subject man to their power; for he is already above them, just as the moon looks down on the landscape. They can only 'bark' and 'bay' at him. That they can do to frighten him. Many fall into this trap, for the moment they reach this threshold and want to cross over into the purely spiritual life while still in the living mortal body, they are seized by the fear that they could now actually physically experience death and die. . . . They withdraw in fright and fall back into this side of life, into the material-worldly state of consciousness. That is why in the ancient initiation rites the candidate was tested for his courage in the face of mortal danger. But our 'magician', who has already passed through all the previous states of consciousness, no longer needs this test. He does not let the keepers of the threshold deter him. He knows that there is no death, only eternal life, and he wishes to enter it at all costs. The wolf still barks at the man of courage but *does not bite him.* He lets him pass through. Only the white dog, symbol of his animal-psychic bonds, remains to be conquered. When the 'magician' has reached the stage where he consciously wishes to cross the threshold and immerse in the ocean of the divine – at this overwhelming moment the image of a loved one, perhaps of his child, springs up from deep within himself and this thought alone is sufficient for the white dog to restrain him with this apparition. He wants to seize him by exploiting love – personal love! But no! Even if he tears himself away from all those for whom he still has a deep personal affection, he knows that he can never lose these people, but will only come closer to them in the spiritual world. Completely merged with God, in a divine UNITY, he will become *one* not only with those he loves, but with the whole universe which also includes the latter. And with his consciousness he bravely continues on his way in the footsteps of the GREAT ONES – into the boundless distance, to immortality, to eternity. He crosses the threshold, nothing remains to daze him, no apparition can hold him back. In his consciousness he goes through the gates of death to find on the other side the long-yearned-for deliverance.

In blessed meditation man may experience all this. In such a state of consciousness man is above everything, just as the moon looks down on the earth. Just as in this picture the crayfish withdraws into the pool, so man, in meditation, withdraws into his divine Self. And as the moon in the dark sky reflects like a mirror the light of the sun to the earth, so man now radiates the light of God to the whole world, to every living creature, to every plant, to every animal and to every human being. He no longer feels any difference between the people to whom he is tied by an earthly blood relationship and those with whom he has a purely spiritual bond. He can see that consanguinity is a purely animal, purely physical bond. If there is no underlying spiritual tie then he has no more kinship with his relatives than with all the other creatures of the world. In death all blood-ties fall away with the body and there remains only the spiritual union in GOD. We then feel in Him our inner union with all that lives, we feel that we stand in our AWARENESS OF SELF in relation with the entire living universe – that we can and do taste the fruits of the TREE OF LIFE.

An old Jewish fable has it that a man asked his neighbour: 'Whom do you love more, your brother or your friend?' And the other answered: 'I love my brother if he has become my friend.' Not the blood relationship, but the spiritual oneness is essential!

At this level of consciousness man crosses the threshold between life and death, from the earthly point of view. From the spiritual point of view, however, this threshold is the border between *death and life*. Physical birth into matter signifies death for the spirit, but birth into the spiritual world, into the *native realm* of the spirit, denotes resurrection and eternal life for the spirit – for the earthly consciousness, on the other hand, death. From the earthly side, the foreground on the divided landscape of tarot card 18 denotes life, and the background death. From the spiritual side, however, the foreground means death and the background resurrection and eternal life in GOD! The 'magician' now passing through here has seen everything '*the other way round*' since tarot card 12!

The person crossing this threshold vanishes as far as his spiritual being is concerned from the ken of earthly men. They still see his body, but his inner being gradually recedes until it is no longer comprehensible to them. It disappears on the path to infinity, to eternity. Now he not only sees everything in reverse, he also sees the transient in all that is earthly, yet he appreciates only the lasting, the intransient, the eternal. And behind all earthly forms, whether plant, animal or man, he sees only the lasting, the absolute, the eternal. In each earthly form he already perceives its future as if it were already present – the transience, the constant change and the ultimate dissolution of everything that is form, its return to where it came from: God. In the case of his own earthly body too he sees the change, the transience, the coming extinction and disappearance from the earthly sphere. Yet he knows now that his true being, his EGO, his SELF, has nothing to do with transience, for his true SELF is eternal, just as GOD is eternal.

Tarot card 18 carries the numerical value 90 which consists of the sum of the digits of the number 18 and the 0, symbol of boundless space. It carries the letter TZADDI. The number 18 consists of the divine number 1 and the number 8. Eight is the falling of the spiritual into matter, thus the mirror-reflection and the eternal cycle of the infinite from the spiritual into the material and back again. Moved by the sight of the Staubbach waterfall in the Lauterbrunnen valley, Goethe divines:

> The soul of man
> Resembleth water:
> From heaven it cometh,
> To heaven it soareth,
> And then again
> To earth descendeth,
> Changing ever.

The free spirit is caught in this endless rotation which signifies its death. If, however, we add the number 8 to the divine number 1, we obtain 9, the number of absolute adjustment and adaptability. At this level each tarot card, therefore each number, contains the symbol of infinity, 0, and thus the two numbers result in the number 90. The number 9 was discussed at the ninth tarot card. It was shown that it stands for 'self-denial' and 'self-effacement'. This number always remains itself, it does not change, no matter how it may be manipulated, it always remains 9 and its adaptability is equally unalterable. Together with the o, the number 9 no longer stands for adaptability to *earthly* powers; rather, as the number 90, it becomes a self-sacrificing and malleable *instrument of God*.

The letter TZADDI designates a border, an end, a goal. TZADDI is a terminal sign referring to all ideas of limitation and release from division and aim. In this instance it symbolises the border between life and death – and death and life. As a hieroglyph TZADDI stands for a pool inhabited by the elemental creatures – nymphs and Tritons. Symbolically speaking it is the pool full of 'living creatures', the water swarming with *living experiences* of the unconscious manifesting itself, i.e. *of the unconscious becoming conscious*. As a letter TZADDI corresponds to the letter TETH, number 9, of the hermit. In hieroglyphics TZADDI and TETH express the same idea, something that offers man shelter and protection, like a roof in the rain; thus his guardian angels.

THE SUN

Numerical Value: 100

Letter: ק KOPH

Here we see the two opposite poles which are also manifested through the two sexes. We have already encountered them on several previous cards; once on tarot card 5 where the two sexes were depicted kneeling together before the high priest; then on tarot card 15 where they were chained to Satan's pedestal as two small devils – one male, the other female. On the fifth card they were both clothed, and even though they touched each other, they were wholly independent, free beings. On tarot card 15, however, they were already naked, they revealed their true being and were tied by heavy rope to an iron ring at the base of Satan's pedestal. Then they were still naked slaves of the Devil.

Now they appear again as two handsome and redeemed young people. They wear only a loin-cloth. Just as on the fifteenth tarot card they revealed their true nature in a naked state – at that time they were still diabolic because of their enslavement by Satan – so now they show their true nature which is pure, healthy and beautiful. The male figure wears a red loin-cloth, thus a positive-masculine, spiritual one; that worn by the female figure is greenish-blue in colour, thus negative-feminine, psychic. This means that in this instance the sexes should be regarded not as a physical-material principle, but as a purely spiritual one. Both figures have golden curls, their colour further enhanced by the rays of the sun. They have joined hands. The male figure holds out his right hand, the female figure her left one. They embrace each other behind their backs with their other arms. They stand in perfectly symmetrical positions which shows that they are equal beings.

The iron ring, to which the figures were chained as devils, has now become a lovely green wreath lying on the ground. The two figures stand side by side within this wreath. Thus again they are joined together but no longer physically, externally, as by Satan, now they are united in the spirit, just as they had complemented each other and formed a unity before Satan separated them. The circle invariably symbolises the spirit, thus they are united by visual symbolism. They have neither worldly clothing nor mortal bodies. Hence this union within the wreath denotes an inner, purely spiritual unity. Those who has reached this level of consciousness carries this purely spiritual unity of the two sexes, in which the two poles rest within each other, *within himself.*

The two figures stand in front of a well-built wall which is both a grave and an alchemist's furnace. It is here that alchemistic processes take place. This grave, this furnace, is the promise that one day something golden, perfect and living will emerge from it. For the time being we merely see that the wall is built of variously coloured bricks, that various energies are therefore at work inside. We already know that these colours symbolise spirituality (red), faith in God (blue) and intellectual powers (yellow).

A big golden sun casts its maturing, warming and penetrating rays on this young couple. It has twelve yellow and twelve red rays. This is an allusion to the twelve-fold partition of heaven, to the twelve signs of the zodiac. The sun radiates wisdom and spirituality. The sun-woman has blue eyes and lovely red lips. Just as on tarot card 18 the moon dominated the whole picture, so in this case does the sun. Without saying a word this sun-woman radiates her friendly warm being to the world around her, thus giving rise to the most violent chemical changes in her vicinity. She also shines upon the grave-like furnace; we may therefore assume that a violent chemical reaction takes place here too. ~~The man~~ *Those* who at the level of consciousness of tarot card 18 crossed the border between death and life – and life and death – has become his own higher Self, which has always been present as his inner voice, as his 'holy spirit'. Now the THOU has become his own EGO. He himself is it! TAT TVAM ASI in the words of the Indian Vedanta philosophy, THOU ART THAT. At the level of consciousness of tarot card 19 man changes from a reflector of light to a source of light. He is no longer a mirror like the moon merely reflecting the light of the sun, as yet unable to radiate its own light and warmth: *he has become the sun, the source of light itself*! The agent of revelation has become a *revealer*. He himself has become the source of the manifestations. He radiates his own divine wisdom and love, his own divine spirituality to the whole world and gilds it with his own golden being. Through his golden Self an entirely new living creature, a new man matures within himself so that his body too is transformed by a chemical process – already in the final stages – and all the metals it contains are turned to gold. Indeed! *He himself* lies in this coffin, in this athanor, and is transformed inside it. The old person will die here in order to give life to a *new* person. As described in the old alchemist books the Phoenix is consumed by fire, but then a magnificent new bird rises from its ashes and soars up into the skies.

Now this no longer happens symbolically, but in *material reality*. Now the person is no longer destroyed symbolically, the human body is transformed, bones and all. This transformation can be *proved and attested chemically*. Like Jesus, Buddha and other god-men, this man carries the two poles, the two sexes spiritually united within himself. The two poles complement each other in this man's spirit. The two sexes are equally strong in his spirit and they are also manifested in his spiritual being. He is both positive and negative and therefore his body too no longer reacts one-sidedly. In his body as in his spirit he is neutral. The other sex has no further influence on his body because he consciously carries both sexes, which complement each other, within himself, just as GOD carries the two poles within himself in a well-balanced state of rest. The ancient Chinese symbol of God – Yang and Yin – shows us the two poles resting within each other in perfect equilibrium.

Since the beginnings of mankind there have been initiates who have known this secret of the chemical transformation of the body and kept it from immature men. They have passed it on only to their disciples. It originates in the Orient and was brought back to Europe in the Middle Ages by the Crusaders. Those who learned it in Europe and handed it on to some of their disciples called themselves Rosicrucians or alchemists. These initiates knew that with the development of his consciousness man also *changes the chemical composition of his body*. The conscious man may *accelerate* this chemical process by various exercises. *Spiritual maturity*, however, is indispensable and that is why this secret must not be revealed to the immature. With this in mind the Rosicrucians concealed their knowledge in mysterious writings and pictures in order nevertheless to rouse the interest of *mature men*.

The symbolic pictorial representations of the Rosicrucians are identical with those of the tarot cards. For instance we frequently find Satan depicted by the Rosicrucians, even in the Masonry which later developed from Rosicrucianism. But we also find other motifs from the tarot cards; the picture of death or of the alchemistic furnace and that of the sexes joining hands in the figure of a man and a woman, often wearing a crown. In particular, the last four cards of the tarot are recognisable in the representations of the Rosicrucians, the alchemists and the Masons. Hence we see that on the nineteenth card the gold, the divine-spiritual solar energy, is developed in the furnace, in this human grave, and that like the Phoenix man will rise out of this athanor, from his own ashes as a resurrected being. We feel here that something of great importance and solemnity happens in this grave-athanor. The ordinary man becomes a *man of magic*.

The spiritual sun lets its own energy, its own gold fall onto the grave-athanor. Thus allusion is made to the secret exercises which can be performed by the spiritually mature man who has already crossed the threshold, in order to accelerate his development and make his body ready to receive and absorb the highest divine frequencies. Just as ordinary iron can be made magnetic, so the ordinary man is made *magical* through this process. The ordinary man who has no light of his own becomes a divine source of light who no longer needs help from anybody but rather *gives* help to every man and living creature.

The first nine cards carried unit numbers, the following nine increased by tens, and the last four increase by hundreds. Tarot card 19 therefore carries the numerical value 100 which consists of the sum of the digits of 19 and of two ciphers, symbols of boundless space. It also carries the letter KOPH.

The number 19 consists of the divine original number 1 and of the 'self-sacrificing' number 9, symbol of the creative negative, which remains itself in every situation, because it always adapts itself perfectly and is therefore the absolute feminine.

The number 9 was discussed thoroughly at the ninth tarot card. Since 9 does not change the base number 1 to which it is added, both numbers together result in the divine original number 1 with the 0, therefore the number 10. 10 is the fulfilment and perfection of creation. It is the return to the source 1, with perfected creation in space in the 0, because it contains the two sexes, the two poles, the number 1, the divine-positive pole, and the number 9, the divine-negative pole. Here, too, man completes his development in creation. He has reached the highest limit, fulfilment and perfection. By the same token he has now also become the number 10. This card carries ten squared, thus 100. Each side of the symbol of matter, therefore each side of the square has become 10. And ten squared is 100.

In hieroglyphics the letter KOPH means a hatchet, a weapon which defends and protects man. It means light, the illumined and animated earth and corresponds to the name Kodesh which in turn means the 'saint'. The latter rules over the stars and the inanimate to which he gives life.

JUDGEMENT

Numerical Value: 200

Letter: ר RESH

In this picture we see an angel in heaven blowing a trumpet. Like the queen of heaven he wears a red and blue dress with yellow edging. He wears a red cap which shows his high spirituality. He has two large wings which enable him to fly through boundless space. He radiates twelve long red and yellow rays to the earth. The number 12 again alludes to the twelvefold division of heaven by the twelve signs of the zodiac. The angel blows a large golden trumpet to show that the time has come when the 'old mortal person' will become the 'new immortal man'. He blows the trumpet to waken the man in the grave to resurrection. This resurrection of the transformed, immortal human being is also indicated by the small red banner hanging from the angel's trumpet. A golden cross in the middle of the flag refers to the transformation of matter – of the material body of the resurrected man. Every metal has been turned to gold in the furnace. As we already know, this furnace is man himself and his spiritual progress effects not merely a symbolical but an actual transformation of his body. Man has risen like Christ from the grave.

On the earth below is the grave where the 'old person' lay and from where the 'new man' now rises. The grave is open. The 'new man' is represented in the picture as a grown-up 'child'. This shows that like the child he carries sex within himself in a dormant state, yet does not identify with it in his consciousness. Christ says to us: 'Except ye . . . become as little children, ye shall not enter into the kingdom of heaven.' These words may be interpreted in several important ways, one of which is that, like children, we should be in a pre-sexual state if we wish to attain the divine state of consciousness and inner peace. We should not be *sexless* and abnormal, just as the child is not abnormal, but perfectly healthy and normal, even though it does not actively manifest sexuality. We can use these powers *for ourselves* and should not expend them for the purpose of endowing a new living creature with life.*

In the picture we therefore see a healthy but childlike man, who, at the moment of rising from the grave-furnace as a new-born and resurrected person, stands there disconcerted and shaken. He is quite simply HERE and NOW. He experiences total presence of the spirit.

To his right and left two figures stand admiring him. A naked man and a naked woman. They symbolise the two sexes. The lower part of their bodies with the sexual organs has been buried *in the ground*. This means that they still expend their sexual urge as prisoners of the earth. Both are normal, healthy people, and yet they are not happy, otherwise they would not watch the man rising out of the grave with such admiration. They know only too well the problems and suffering caused by sex life, how men are enslaved by it and forfeit their freedom, and that sexual pleasure is short-lived. When the glands grow tired what remains of the erotic magic? – Only enslavement, only lost freedom. These captive people look at the new, resurrected, childlike man with admiration and longing. They are already 'seekers' yearning for redemption and they envy and admire the man who has found and experienced it. Both of them have their hands folded in prayer showing their reverence and admiration for this divine act, for this transformed

* cf. E. Haich, *Sexual Energy and Yoga* (Allen & Unwin, 1972).

man, re-born and resurrected in the spirit and in the body, who
lives in a perpetual, undisturbed state of happiness. They already know the uncertain and inconstant quality of the
happiness afforded by sexuality. And our spirit, which is
eternal, *longs for eternal, everlasting joys and happiness*!

At this level of consciousness we have the strange experience
which every human being must go through at the moment of
death. Those who have already been 'on the other side' but
were resuscitated, report that they experienced the 'Last Judgement'. The moment the spirit – the EGO – 'shuffles off this
mortal coil', the many impressions accumulated in the unconscious in the course of a long or short life are released, and
suddenly, simultaneously, penetrate the consciousness. We
see our whole life telescoped before us, just as a piece of music
is present in its entirety on a gramophone record. Yet both
the record and life can only be experienced *in time*. In the same
way as the gramophone needle passes over the surface of the
record from start to finish, so we have had to pass through our
life in time from beginning to end. In death, however, we
experience a state in which our life is no longer perceived *in*
time and space, but *beyond* time and space, and in which experiences and impressions simultaneously penetrate our consciousness. The 'resurrected man' experiences this condition while
still in the physical life, in the physical state. He must settle
accounts with his life like the man who has just died, as if he
were to experience the whole thing once more, *not in time* but
all at once. Just as we can survey a landscape from above, in
its entirety, without having to wander through it all on foot!
In this state we see everything at once in exactly the way it
has happened to us. In so doing it is no longer possible, as it
was in real life, to see a thing through rose-coloured spectacles,
to disguise it or invent excuses for oneself or others. No!
We must let everything pass before our mind's eye exactly
as it has happened, and experience it anew without embellish-
ment, disguise or masking. We must look the facts in the eye
whether we like them or not, we must re-witness and re-

experience all our deeds stripped bare, exactly as they were. We must also acknowledge what led us to these actions. We will be confronted with all the motives for our words and deeds, and, as it says in the Bible, the sheep will be separated from the goats, the sheep placed on the right and the goats on the left. We must judge everything that we have thought, said and done, and suffer the judgement to be enacted on ourselves. We are not judged by a GOD outside us, but it is we ourselves who speak our own verdict. But the person at this level is relieved at having paid off his debts to all men. The effort to make progress has not been in vain. It has been worth his pains for all accounts are settled. The levels of consciousness of the previous cards have already shown him what attitude he must adopt towards himself and other people, whom, as Christ taught, he should regard and love as 'himself', if he does not wish to cause a new karma to arise. He has already crossed the great threshold and no guardian could restrain him from it. Now he only casts a last look at his life and, free, without debt, he raises himself above everything, raises himself above the earth with all its joys and sorrows. Even if he cannot yet shed his mortal body, he already sees everything from above, as if hovering above this world, just as the angel hovers over his head, above the world. He sees clearly why he is in this world, what God still wishes of him, and does everything that he himself considers proper, in order one day *to bring this life to a creditable conclusion*. He no longer needs to hear from the inner voice what he still has to do in life, because HE HIMSELF HAS BECOME THIS INNER VOICE! He no longer has any conscience, he can no longer have any pangs of conscience, because HE HAS BECOME HIS OWN CONSCIENCE!

At the level of tarot card 13, man was destroyed as a person and awoke in the spirit. He realised that his ego is not a material, isolated being, but that with the word 'I' he designates the spirit above his person. As a result of this awakening, he had to come to grips with many things, in particular with sexuality. This he did at the level of tarot card 15. He had to learn to convert sexual energy into creative power. Then he learned to control and to pass on his creative powers. He had to learn how to radiate love to all living creatures, just as the sun radiates light and warmth to every living creature. In addition, these new powers changed and transformed his body; he was re-born in the body too, and now, at the present level, he experiences perfect resurrection.

Thus man has freed himself from his grave, from the misconception that he must live imprisoned in the mortal body, and he has experienced resurrection while still in this earthly life. It is true that his body still dwells in the world of matter, but his consciousness stands above it; he is no longer a physical being, he no longer has a personal 'I' – an *apparent ego* – rather, he has become one with the SPIRIT OF THE UNIVERSE, with the absolute higher SELF OF THE UNIVERSE, which has released him from this misconception. He has experienced the 'mystical marriage', the '*unio mystica*'. HIS CONSCIOUSNESS HAS BECOME ONE AND IDENTICAL WITH THE DIVINE, WITH THE TRUE SELF. He also sees everything from the 'other', from the 'reverse' side, he looks BACK from there, because he has already crossed the threshold. He feels that his feet have been hitherto chained to the ground and that for a long time he was unable to free himself. Now the fetters are loosed and cast off. For even if they existed only in his imagination, that is *the very reason* why they were a *reality* for him. Now nothing restrains him any longer. He can spread his wings – which had always been there but could not be used because he was not aware of them – and fly into spaceless freedom, into timeless eternity.

Tarot card 20 carries the numerical value 200 which consists of the number 20 and the 0, symbol of boundless space. It carries the letter RESH.

At this level man is aware that he has found the two worlds which he had sought already at the second level but had been unable to attain. He feels at home in both worlds, in both of them he experiences his *own* world. He sees that there is no such thing as 'the world beyond' versus 'this world'.

Both form a unity, for this world has *no existence* without the next world. This world is sometimes a very imperfect manifestation of the next world. *Man's Self has always been in the world beyond and always remains there whether it is embodied or not.* Without the spirit there is no LIFE in matter. Now he understands everything that the high priestess kept from him by not raising the curtain before the shrine. There is no plurality, there is only one single, sacred UNITY: GOD.

Thus man achieved the development so wonderfully described by Gustav Meyrink in his work, *Das grüne Gesicht*: 'Like Janus he was able to look into the other world and at the same time into this, our world, and clearly distinguish their respective constituent objects:

> *he was here and yonder*
> *a living man.'*

In hieroglyphics the letter RESH means the human head and according to applied symbolism it means the 'return' to the divine world, just as on this card, at this level, man has risen again in the divine world, has therefore returned there.

THE FOOL

Numerical Value: 300

Letter: ש SHIN

On this card we see a strange man, apparently without a care in the world, wandering around in even stranger clothing. On his head we see a large turban composed of fairly broad coloured stripes. It looks as if these stripes were radiating from his head. We see here the most important colours, yellow, green, red and a narrow white stripe. We know that red denotes spirituality, green goodwill and love of humanity, yellow intellectual powers, through which spirituality is manifested, and white, purity. The jacket is made up of the same colours with the addition of blue, i.e. devotion and faith in God. The back of his head and his neck are covered with a green cloth, so that neither his hair nor his ears are visible. His face is bare: the FOOL does not wear a moustache, but where the cloth ends he has a narrow brown beard framing his face. Therefore we really see nothing of his head because it is entirely covered. Nor do we really see his face. This face is much too big in relation to the size of his body. It cannot be his own face, it is a *mask*. Yet even the mask is scarcely visible because the FOOL holds *up* his face – his mask; he looks up to higher worlds, to heaven, where he is at home, and not to the ground. His face is therefore visible only to the person who lifts his own face up.

The magician's wand has become a simple walking-stick which he holds in his right hand. The stick is red, thus symbolising spiritual help on the path. In his left hand he holds a narrow green club, similar to a stick. Although he carries it in his left hand, he lays it across his right shoulder. He has brought everything over from the negative to the positive side. He has nothing else on his left side, he even holds his left hand to the right. He carries a small bag hanging from the green, club-like stick. In this he carries all his possessions. The colour of the bag indicates that its contents too are only spiritual.

The fool wears yellow hose and brown shoes. But the hose have been torn down by a strange animal so that his posterior is naked. The animal still bites his leg but the fool pays no attention whatever, as if he did not feel anything at all. He continues on his way unconcerned and calm, looks up to the sky, carries his little bag and does not pay heed to animals which bite him from behind. He is equally unconcerned about the animals which lie in wait for him. Behind a beam a crocodile waits for him. But he is apparently afraid of the fool and does not dare attack him.

Between his legs we again see the red flower. It is open, but inclines its head so that no one can see into the heart of its cup. The fool no longer shows his treasures to anyone.

Who is this fool?

This FOOL is man who has passed through the most advanced stages of human development on earth and has reached the highest level. His consciousness has united with the divine. Yet in so doing he has removed himself so far in spirit from his fellow-men that nobody understands him any longer. Already as the HANGED MAN he saw everything the other way round; but even if he saw everything in this way, he did so from a *human point of view*. Now that he has crossed the threshold between the two worlds and finally died in the grave-furnace as a mortal human being to rise to a new life as a heavenly being, he can no longer see anything from the human standpoint. Not even earthly life. He has brought everything over to the right, spiritual side; he sees everything from a divine eternal point of view. He no longer sees any difference between the finite and the infinite, between the mortal and the immortal. He sees clearly – even if it is applied to himself – that only the forms change, but that nothing has a beginning and an end. There is nothing that *could* die. No! *Even if we wanted to or had to, we cannot die.* There is no death! There is only eternal life, eternal transformation and rotation. LIFE, LIFE everywhere we look! A dying plant, a dying animal or a dying man have only reached a bourn where they will change their earthly garment and don a new one. What lives – the Self – cannot die because it *has never been born*. And what has been born, matter, the body, cannot die either, because the earthly garment, the body, has never had independent life, it has never lived. The body of a plant, an animal or a man lives merely because the spirit – the Self – is embodied in it and manifests *its own life* through the body. Matter, the body, as such, does not live, and when the Self leaves the body, there remains only a decaying, dead form. Many people have a panic fear of death, but the fool is no more afraid of it than a person who undresses at night to go to bed is afraid of sleep. Is he dead because he is not wearing clothes any longer? Or are the clothes now dead and less alive than during the time when he was inside them? Even when they were worn they were not alive. They merely complied with and imitated the movements which their wearer made in them. Now that he has taken them off, they have grown neither more nor less alive than they have always been. The FOOL regards life only from the standpoint of the divine. How could people understand him who pursue merely the gratification of the body, who consider it more important than anything else and regard it as the single goal in life? For the fool none of this is important at all. In the activities of his fellow-men he participates only as far as is absolutely necessary, for he does not wish to stir up trouble and he knows that it is all completely unimportant anyway. He sees men clearly, he also understands them for he knows that, at the level of development where ordinary people stand, they *cannot help being like that.* But people do not understand his point of view. And the fool does not enter into discussion. He does not want to be right for he knows *that anyone at his level of development is right*! It is only a matter of time when those people who do not understand him at present and regard him as a fool will themselves reach this level, be as little understood and regarded as fools.

Those who cannot yet understand him are displeased that he does not offer any explanations about himself or discuss with them. They want to see his 'face' and get to know his character. And what happens? These people cannot see his true being, there is no way of allowing them insight into his true being. They could never follow him into his world, because they would not yet be able to sustain these vibrations. These people have no idea that 'his world' even exists and that it is the absolute reality. They do not know that theirs is only a world of visions, a dream. Thus primitive worldly people cannot see him in his spiritual reality, they only see that part which is visible in the material world; they only see how he lives in the realm of matter and what he does there visibly and tangibly. Thus they see him only from his *purely material* side. Since time immemorial the material side of man has been symbolised by the organ which serves to eject the waste matter, the impurities, from the body, thus by the anus. Thus the inquisitive bite of the 'animal' primitive men who want to 'bite into' the living flesh of the fool, merely renders his posterior, his purely material side, naked and visible. The curious see *only this side* of him. They can watch when he rises or goes to bed, what he eats and drinks or how he behaves outwardly at his place of work.

All this can be observed by the maliciously curious. But this breed of mortals has no inkling of his spiritual being. And just as animals tear apart other animals if they are not like themselves, so these primitive people want to tear apart the

FOOL. Yet they will never be able to see HIM. Just as they could not see Christ, only kill his body.

Thus, whoever has reached the goal must continue whether his primitive fellow-men 'bite' him or not. He knows that he always remains the same and no matter what others may think or say of him, he *cannot* and *will* not change. He *is* how and what he *is*! And he has long forgotten vanity! Vanity, envy, hate and other human qualities belong to the human standpoints. For a long time, however, he has seen everything only from a divine point of view. He continues unconcerned and unimpeded on his way. And if he hears people calling him a fool behind his back, he is not in the least offended. On the one hand he takes it as a matter of course, on the other hand he cannot harbour any resentment and lives at peace with his fellow-men. He knows that they are as yet unable to think differently. He leaves them alone, for one must not pluck unripe fruits from the tree, otherwise they *could never ripen*.

This card does not have a number, but it carries the letter SHIN to which the number 21 belongs in cabbalism. The numerical value 300 must have arisen from the number 21 with two ciphers. The number 3 with two ciphers, thus 300, is obtained by multiplying the divine number 3 with the square of 10, which is the fulfilment of creation in the universe. This card cannot be considered in isolation and therefore does not carry a number. It is only the external image of man whose inner side is symbolised by the next tarot card, 22. This last card, the WORLD, shows the inner nature of the FOOL, his inner state of consciousness. He does not value wealth and secular power which primitive men prize above all else, but spiritual riches, the very existence of which is not even known to primitive men. He is therefore a FOOL! Yet this FOOL bears *within himself* what is shown by the last card, divine ALL-CONSCIOUSNESS!

Even though this card is unnumbered, we feel that it is the twenty-first tarot card and that it is connected with the number 21 because it carries the numerical value 300 and the letter

SHIN. This letter is a corner-stone of the alphabet. According to the Cabbala, God set the letter SHIN as king over the element fire. It is therefore fire, the fire of the spirit, of the creative principle, of Logos. Moses beheld God in a *burning* bush, thus in fire. Suddenly he saw that life – GOD – is manifested in the material world as fire. But the spirit of fire which the earthly, visible fire merely manifests, yet is *not* itself this *visible fire*, is LIFE ITSELF, is GOD HIMSELF! – And Christ says in the Bible: 'I baptise you with fire . . .' HE, Christ, is the fire and the LIFE. He himself says: 'I am the LIFE.' If the name of the omnipotent, impersonal God consists of all the vowels and the letter H, through which God breathes life, the Self, into man, then we obtain the following name for GOD: IEHOUA (Yod He Vau He). If we now insert the letter SHIN, which means the fire of life, in the middle of the name of the *impersonal* God, we obtain the word IEHOSHUA. This is the name of the *personal* God, of God incarnate. For in the original Hebrew language the name Jesus is Jehoshua. Only in the West is he known as Jesus.

We understand the importance of the letter SHIN because it is the fire with which Christ, the higher Self, baptises us, initiates us into LIFE. This card represents the Christ-man!

The state depicted on this card is fatal for the immature man. The mature man with his universal, all-embracing self-awareness becomes identical with God at this level and lives according to the inner divine laws while still recognising the secular laws. The immature man, however, lacking all-consciousness, does not yet recognise the divine laws or even the secular ones. He loses his inner balance, plunges into the abyss, into the void, and in the language of ordinary people, he becomes mentally ill. To the immature man this card means hell, to the mature person, the God-man, it means heaven.

Tarot card 12, the HANGED MAN, is linked with the number 30 (the sum of the digits of 12 is 3, plus the 0, symbol of space). It was for thirty pieces of silver that Judas betrayed Christ. This card, the FOOL, carries the same number, but takes on cosmic significance with the second 0, thus with 300.

The HANGED MAN is still a *man*, the FOOL is the GOD-MAN who has attained universal consciousness. We see the link between the number 300 and the letter SHIN. Both denote GOD-MEN.

The FOOL is a man who HAS BECOME ONE in his consciousness with LOGOS, with CHRIST, with LIFE!

THE WORLD

Numerical Value: 400

Letter: ת Tav

Looking at this card we sense that something universal, something cosmic, is represented here. In the centre there is a beautiful woman in whom we recognise the queen of heaven after her various transformations into 'Justice', 'Love', 'Balance' and the lovely naked woman on the picture of the 'Stars'. She is again naked in this picture; she does not need to veil her body from mortal eyes, because she is now in her native country, in the universe where she is at home. She wears a narrow red cloth with which she symbolises her high spirituality. She has golden, curly hair symbolising her intellectual powers and in her left hand she holds two magic wands. One of them has a red sphere at the top, the other a green one. We already know that these two spheres denote the positive and the negative charge of the two wands. Like the king of heaven on tarot card 4 and the hanged man on tarot card 12, the queen of heaven has her legs crossed, the cross being the symbol of the material world. As already stated, she is the maternal aspect of God which rules over the material side of the universe; she is the great MOTHER, she is NATURE. The magic wands are her laws, which prevail and operate inflexibly throughout the entire universe.

She stands within a large green wreath. It is the same wreath that lies on the ground on tarot card 19 encircling the two young people. In the present instance the wreath denotes cosmic, infinite space, it is the great CIPHER. This wreath is represented on some tarot cards designed and illustrated by other artists as the serpent biting its own tail, which symbolises infinity and rotation.

Outside the wreath we see four signs of the zodiac: the lion, bull, cherub and eagle. We also know these four corner-points of heaven from the Bible, the three animals and the angel in the vision of Ezekiel.* The same four creatures were depicted on the Ark of the Covenant.

The four evangelists, too, are linked with these signs of the zodiac: the lion with Mark, the bull with Luke, the cherub with Matthew and the eagle with John, the redeemed scorpion, Judas.

This picture symbolises the universe, the immeasurable cosmos. The man who has attained this level has become one with GOD in his consciousness. He may say what Christ says in the Bible: 'I and my Father are one.' He is a God-man. His position towards GOD is no longer a dualistic one: he is now in a monistic state with Him. He can no longer pray to an *external* God, for he realises that God is to be found only on the *inward* path, on the path to the ego, in the depths of his own being. This path begins with man's perception of his personal, little 'ego' and his growing awareness in this 'apparent-ego'.

Then he begins the gradual process of acquiring self-know-ledge and discovers that everything he had hitherto regarded as his own Self was only a conglomeration of various drives, instincts and desires *plus reason*. He discovers that his little, personal 'ego' is merely an 'apparent-ego' and that his true being is involved with it only inasmuch as it gave the little 'apparent-ego' individual life. When man reaches the stage where he has realised and become conscious of this, he has

* cf. E. Haich, *Initiation*, op. cit.

already partly renounced identification with the little physical-material 'apparent-ego'. He has grown in his consciousness and come closer to his true being, his true EGO.

He continues his inner struggle and climbs ever higher in his consciousness on the great Jacob's ladder. Fate helps him by giving him experiences and trials which bring him increasingly closer to himself, no matter how much these trials may cause him suffering and pain. He must learn to see his personal 'ego' more and more from above, like an indifferent onlooker. He passes through all the levels symbolised here by the tarot cards until he *becomes* his own higher SELF, his true BEING. It is not enough merely to *understand* these inner truths rationally. At that stage he is still far from *realisation*. He must reach the level where he is nothing else but a naked, divine being completely free of physical-material qualities. In every respect and position he can only be himself, *must* be himself, *because he cannot be different*! He has been healed of the disorders of the soul which are called covetousness, envy, vanity and thirst for power. They were never the qualities of his true Self. Now he *must* and *can only* manifest divine qualities, because he *has become divine*. If he were to behave as an ordinary, personal man in order not to infuriate other people, he would afterwards despise himself to such an extent that he would prefer to withdraw completely from society so that he would not always be misunderstood and continually obliged to explain his reasons for saying this or doing that. Yet that is not the only reason why such a person withdraws. On the long path to the SELF, his sense-organs have reached such a degree of sensitivity that he sees right through other people. And even though he understands them and bears no resentment, he suffers greatly by having to watch his fellow-men destroy themselves with a wrong way of life.

He also knows that if he tells them the truth a hundred times, they will heed him as little as they heeded Christ, preferring to hasten to their own destruction. He prefers not to have to watch this and he goes away. But his super-sensitive organs of perception also cause him great distress, because the eating and drinking, smells and sounds of other people are a heavy strain on his delicate nerves. These people withdraw completely from the worldly life, from their fellow-men, unless God has imposed on them the test of *having* to live with other men in order to fulfil their task. Since this is very hard to achieve in Europe, they go to another part of the world and live there like the others who can no longer endure it in the world. We could give many instances, but that is unnecessary. Apart from those known to every seeker from books or hearsay, such as Rama Krishna, Shivapuribaba or Ramana Maharshi, there are others known only to few. The present author knows several instances of Western men and women (for example a so-called society lady) who travelled to India, had their hair cut and continued their lives as insignificant and modest pilgrims. Once you have met such people and talked to them, and thus experienced their harmony and peace with which civilised man is totally unacquainted, it is obvious why they have withdrawn from the 'world'.

No one is entitled to criticise such people. The standards by which they live are different from those of worldly men. They already have inherent in them the state of the 'hanged man' and of the 'fool'. They have no further need for all the things the worldly man still believes to be indispensable. They do not need to travel here or there because they already know that the world is equally beautiful anywhere if we behold the *revealer* – GOD – behind every form, in every manifestation. Such a person does not need to go to museums and art galleries to see wonderful representations of the beauties of the world. Not that he would not appreciate the talents and revelations of the artists, no, he even values them much more than ordinary men. But he knows that every piece of music, every painting, every statue is merely a *partial manifestation a part of the whole.* The smallest piece of work, still more the different arts, are the way to the goal, to the *whole*, to the development to perfection, to one's SELF, to GOD! Yet these people do not need that any more; they have arrived at the goal; they have become perfection, the whole, GOD. Why should they therefore manifest only a *part*, if they *have become the whole*? Moses, Jesus, Buddha and the other titanic spirits who reached the goal did not compose music, paint pictures, carve figures or, like David, dance before the altar in order to manifest God. These people know that all art is a divine manifestation when it emerges from the human heart, according to the stage man has reached. But these titans no longer require partial manifestations, they have reached the goal, they have become *the source of all art, as well as the source of all love. And for that very reason they themselves do not feel love any more. Love is the urge for unity. If, however, a man has become* ONE *with the universe, if he has attained* UNITY, *how should he then still feel the urge for unity?* They have come home, they dwell in GOD. Their consciousness has become one with BEING.

Tarot card 22 carries the numerical value 400 which has arisen from the sum of the digits of the number 22, thus 4, multiplied by the square of 10, thus 100. It also carries the letter TAV.

The number 4 carries hidden in itself the divine perfection of creation, the number 10. For if we add the numbers to 4, we obtain the number 10 ($1+2+3+4 = 10$!). The numerical value 400, the number 4 with the two ciphers, symbolises in number mysticism the whole material Creation, the entire universe with the Creator, with GOD. The number 10 is correctly represented as follows:

The woman, the maternal aspect of God, thus God as 'mother', Isis or Kali, is the number 1 on this picture and the wreath is the infinite circle, the universe. Behind the woman who is the visible aspect of God, Nature, we also feel the masculine-feminine aspect of God, the invisible, nameless and unrevealed deity. The Cabbalists call this aspect of God EN-SOPH and the Hindus, PARABRAHMA.

TAV has the same hieroglyphic meaning as DALETH – card 4 – and means the 'womb'. We understand why this letter means the man who has attained the goal. He has reached the very depths, the WOMB of Creation. He has reached the heart of God. This letter is at the same time the symbol of man himself, because man is the purpose and perfection of the entire visible Creation.

Conclusion

We have tried to describe the Greater Arcana of the tarot pack, the twenty-two levels of consciousness, as handed down to us in symbolic representations by the initiates of ancient times. We are convinced that through this book many of our readers will recognise in the cards their own states of consciousness, either the state in which they find themselves at present or one they have experienced in the past. It is a common occurrence that someone with whom we have once discussed these cards comes again years later and tells us with great amazement that, long after he had forgotten all about them, he suddenly experienced an inner state in which he recognised a certain card and only then fully understood its meaning. There have even been people who, never having heard of these cards, yet told me about a spiritual state unmistakably represented by a tarot card. For instance, they experienced the 'Hanged Man', the 'Lightning-Struck Tower' or 'Death'. Some people also felt that they were standing at a cross-road or that they were lying in a grave and rose from it again. Indeed: the 'initiates' did not represent these pictures accidentally and from their imagination, rather, they knew very well that a certain spiritual state is revealed in every man in a quite definite and identical inner image. These pictures sometimes have such a powerful effect that they are projected outwardly, that is to say, they are seen and heard like an outward experience. The tarot cards are also identical with certain dream-images which manifest themselves to many people in one and the same way. There have been attempts to interpret these identical dream-images recurring with different people. In interpreting dream-images, however, we encounter certain fundamental difficulties. The dreams do not usually show pictures of individual tarot cards, but mixtures of them. Therefore one cannot establish a general schematic interpretation for the many variations of these mixed dream-images. When interpreting dreams it is necessary to question the dreamer and to analyse him in order to gain insight into his whole situation. Only then is it possible to understand why this person's unconscious manifested this particular dream, why precisely this mixture of images was dreamt. The tarot cards are the basic elements of the dream-images and not mixtures of them. And to explain and interpret basic elements individually is easily possible.

The purpose of these cards is therefore not merely to improve and help ourselves, but rather to arouse the attention and interest of the serious expert, of the unprejudiced psychologist, and to open his eyes to this magnificent heritage from ancient times. Moses, one of the greatest prophets of all time, received the pictures from the great Egyptian initiates and handed them on as religious treasure to his people, the Jews. If Moses esteemed these cards so highly as to regard them as religious treasure, then the serious psychologist should certainly also be able to discover their profound inner value. Until very recently the method of treatment of the great Chinese doctors, acupuncture, was regarded with contempt in the West. Today, many Western doctors who had the courage to experiment with something unknown are applying this method with great success. Thus psychologists and psychiatrists might also become interested in the tarot cards and find in them a wonderful means for analysing healthy and sick people and if necessary for re-establishing their psychic equipoise. Mental disorders may be diagnosed by the Szondi, Wartegg, Koch and Rorschach tests. In the same way a great deal of time and analytical work can be saved with the help of the tarot cards, since they very quickly provide one with the image of a human soul.

The levels of consciousness depicted by the tarot cards are experienced sooner or later by all men and the experiences invariably correspond to the pictures on the cards. The levels, however, are seldom experienced in the sequence in which the cards occur. Usually they are experienced in random order, that is to say, in the order of the person's development. Life has many aspects and each man's fate is different; we do not develop identically according to a definite pattern. One man reaches maturity in some respect sooner than another. For that reason, too, the sequence of the experiences differs so greatly. One cannot lay down general rules nor expect the levels of development to be experienced in the sequence of the tarot cards. Some remain for a longer period at the same level, afterwards passing through several levels in succession. Another man begins development very quickly and experiences the states of several cards one after the other, then suddenly remains for a long time in the same state. Each of us brings a great number of experiences from our previous life. One person has passed through many levels, another has experienced less in his past life and will have to catch up on what he has missed in this life. This is what explains the great differences which occur between one individual and another. It is, however, evident that the first card, the first dawning of consciousness, must necessarily be the beginning of the series of the states of consciousness. Without this initial coming to consciousness man is merely an animal plus reason and cannot experience further states of consciousness. It is therefore clear that at the very outset he must become aware of his Self and observe that he is *here* and *now*. He must therefore experience the absolute *presence* and absolute *present*. Only after this can he have further states of consciousness. *States of consciousness* can be experienced then only by a person who has already become *conscious*.

Other tarot cards again are so closely connected that they have to follow each other directly. Thus it happens that some states are experienced in the order in which the cards occur. For instance, after a person has been transformed in the coffin, it must follow as a matter of course that he rises out of the grave and is resurrected. Thus as an inner state, tarot card 20 must inevitably follow tarot card 19. Or there is the case of a person who has experienced true selfless 'love', thus the greatest and most irresistible power in the world, because God is love. Thereupon he must necessarily become the 'hanged man' because other people still see everything from a selfish standpoint, the point of view of those who have fallen from Paradise, thus the other way round from the person who sees the world in the light of selfless love. Yet before and after these states others can suddenly and unexpectedly arise which should have occurred only much later or much earlier. And if man is not mature enough for them, he may react abnormally. Then he experiences these 'cards' as an 'abnormal' state. For instance, it can happen that the level of the 'Lightning-Struck Tower' is experienced. Something happens to him which affects him at his most sensitive point – destiny strikes at this point precisely because it is the most sensitive one – and this event ruins him morally or financially in society, disrupting his whole life. If he has not already experienced the level of the 'Wheel of Fortune' at which he learned to see everything, including his own fate, from a higher objective point of view, then it may occur that he reacts quite wrongly to this stroke of fate. He then loses his self-confidence and no longer believes in himself or even in other people. If, in addition to this, he has not yet reached the level of tarot card 11, then he also does not yet know universal love as the highest power. He still lacks the strength to understand and pardon those who may pursue him and wish to hurt him. He will probably hate them and want to take revenge, and may start a long feud. In so doing he only manages to make himself ridiculous and hurts himself still further.

It is an old Egyptian truth that the immature man must not raise the veil of the mysterious Isis – the figure on tarot card 2 – otherwise he would lose his sanity. That which helps a mature man to even greater maturity and 'knowledge' only makes immature men confused and ill. If we observe and concern ourselves with people, we shall see that this is true. We are all different from one another precisely because, in symbolical terms, we are different mixtures of the tarot cards. Yet it also happens that an emotionally disturbed or neurotic person suddenly is restored to health by experiences which move him deeply. Indeed, he has suddenly experienced the missing states of consciousness – the missing cards. The gaps in him have been closed and thus he is able to adopt the correct point of view. It is in exactly this field that an experienced psychiatrist could make use of the tarot cards to effect cures. Only a few experiments would be necessary in order to recognise the profound content and inner significance of these cards. In the course of these he will see clearly which level a person has attained and which level he may have experienced too early or too late. The psychiatrist will also see to which further state he must help someone if he wishes to preserve or restore his spiritual well-being. Of course, a skilled psychiatrist perceives not merely the inner state and the whole character of those who seek help from him, but to a certain extent also their future destiny. For every mental state provokes destiny into reacting with a stroke of fate designed to help man proceed to the next level of development. The psychiatrist will therefore also be able to give some good advice concerning future destiny.

Everyone may of course use these cards, examine them, recognise his own inner states and thus himself, and if necessary set his soul in order. All this can be done without any harmful consequences and even very profitably. God manifests himself through everything, through crystals, plants, animals and through man, according to the level of consciousness he has reached. God manifests himself not merely through living things, but through simply everything. Through colours and sounds, through ideas and thoughts, through letters and numbers, through physical and mathematical laws, through heavenly bodies and through the atom. Anyone who sees the divine essence, divine manifestation and divine laws in all things, is also able to examine and engage in the 'secret' sciences to which the tarot belongs. A mature person will see and come to know the divine thread running through the whole universe. In himself, too, he will behold a revelation of God and will see himself as a divine agent of manifestation. In EVERYTHING, in sciences both known and as yet unknown, he will always find only GOD.

It is the purpose of this book to arouse interest in our own inner development and in our own level of consciousness on the great Jacob's ladder. With the help of these wonderful cards, which have profound inner meaning, every man can look into his soul and learn more about himself, thereby coming closer to himself – to God. We therefore place in each person's hand a wonderful aid to the acquisition of self-knowledge!

For knowledge of the Self means KNOWLEDGE OF GOD!

Phoenix 146

Holy Spirit 146

Thou art That! 146
Tat two asi

AURORA PRESS

THE ELISABETH HAICH SERIES

Through books such as *Initiation*, Elisabeth Haich has become world famous for her profound understanding of the human soul. The Yoga schools she set up in Europe with Selvarajan Yesudian have become internationally renowned.

WISDOM OF THE TAROT
Wisdom of the Tarot relates the path of higher consciousness through the color, shape and symbolic forms on the 22 cards. Detailed study of a Tarot card may release instinctive awareness of each level towards the Light. When studied individually, a card may reveal the necessary steps to find one's essential path. Included are 5 color gold Tarot cards.
Paper 174pp.   **$12.50**

SEXUAL ENERGY & YOGA
This book is to introduce the concept of transmuting the physical emotional psychic mental energy people normally disperse in sexual activity for the purpose of uniting their bodies in their higher Self or God.
Paper 160pp   **$6.95**

THE EAR
Gateway to Balancing the Body
A Modern Guide to Ear Acupuncture
Mario Wexu, D. Ac.
This is the first complete modern textbook of ear acupuncture. Anatomical descriptions with detailed charts clearly illustrate how to locate and use over 300 ear points, both alone and in combination with body points, to treat and prevent illness. An excellent repertory listing 150 diseases facilitates an indepth understanding of this incredible and valuable healing art.
Cloth 203pp.   **$30.00**

COLOR THERAPY
Dr. Reuben Amber
This comprehensive book enumerates the myriad ways we can consciously choose to use color to influence our body, mind, and soul to promote balanced health and well being. No other book includes as thorough a historical survey of Color Therapies along with specific applications of color in all facets of life.
Paper 207pp.   **$9.95**

HOW COSMIC & ATMOSPHERIC ENERGIES INFLUENCE YOUR HEALTH
Dr. Michel Gauquelin
A unique exploration by psychologist and statistician Dr. Michel Gauquelin, of the tremendous influence of the cycle of the seasons, range of climates, cosmic clocks, Lunar Cycles, & Sunspots on the complex balance of mental and physical health.
Paper 224pp.   **$8.95**

SELF HEALING, YOGA AND DESTINY
Designed to reconnect you with the Divine, the concepts within this book explain the attitudes necessary for the path back to one's Self. Based on many years personal experience, the author creates a vehicle to realize the essential source of Life, especially in relation to illness and self healing.
Paper 80pp.   **$4.95**

THE DAY WITH YOGA
A different creative energy is at work on each day of the week. In this book Elisabeth Haich has carefully chosen and collected quotations which show us how we can attune to the cosmic vibrations of each day.
Paper 96pp.   **$3.95**

CHART INTERPRETATION —
Astrology and Psychology
Doris Hebel
A compilation of articles on Chart Interpretation, covering Elements, aspects, hemisphere emphasis, retrogrades, stations, parental indicators, and case histories.
Paper 64pp.   **$5.**

SYNASTRY
Understanding Human Relations
Through Astrology *Ronald Davison*
This book contains the first comprehensive survey of the various techniques of horoscope comparison.

The author has discovered "The Relationship Horoscope," an entirely new way of charting in a single horoscope the relationship between two people. He also introduces new methods of determining the quality of that relationship.
Paper 352pp.   **$10.95**

AWAKEN HEALING ENERGY THROUGH THE TAO
Mantak Chia
This unique book reveals the ancient Taoist secret of circulating internal energy through acupuncture meridians, for physical, psychological and spiritual health. Written in clear, easy to understand language and illustrated with many detailed diagrams that aid the development of a powerful energetic flow.
Paper 224pp.   **$10.95**

AURORA PRESS

Barbara Somerfield is pleased to announce the birth of Aurora Press, a company devoted to publishing books that catalyze personal growth, balance and transformation.

Aurora Press will provide a publishing vehicle for an innovative synthesis of ancient wisdom with twentieth century resources.

Aurora books specialize in astrology, tarot, the healing arts, color therapy, acupuncture, and the emerging global consciousness.

THE DANE RUDHYAR SERIES

We are particularly proud to publish the books of Dane Rudhyar, internationally recognized astrologer, composer, poet, artist and philosopher who initiated the concept of a humanistic and transpersonal approach to life.

THE PLANETARIZATION OF CONSCIOUSNESS

The Planetarization of Consciousness is Rudhyar's major philosophical work, the concentrated outcome of a lifetime of thinking concerning the most basic problems of human existence and the meaning of the radical social-cultural and psychological crisis mankind is experiencing.
Paper 320pp.   **$9.95**

THE GALACTIC DIMENSION OF ASTROLOGY

The Sun is Also a Star
A deepened understanding of Uranus, Neptune and Pluto can guide us towards experiencing the galactic level of consciousness. The "challenge of galacticity" to humanistic astrology releases new perspectives when applied to individual horoscopes. His new interpretations of the trans-Saturnian planets provide a vehicle to transform how we use astrology in our daily lives, and for the evolving planet we live on.
Paper 224pp.   **$7.95**

ASTROLOGICAL INSIGHTS INTO THE SPIRITUAL LIFE

Astrological Insights provides a penetrating, sensitive, poetic and visual insight into the 12 qualities required for the spiritual life, for Astrologers and non-astrologers alike. Using the astrological signs and houses, Rudhyar builds a framework for impregnating the seeker with an awareness of how to use basic life challenges, as a process through which an individual human being evolves. Twelve exquisite artistic renderings evoke the archetypal, intuitive level of each sign.
Paper 160pp.   **$7.95**

AN ASTROLOGICAL TRYPTICH

In *Tryptich* Rudhyar extracts from traditional astrology a great wealth of psychological and spiritual meaning. New interpretations of the zodiacal signs, houses and planets shed light on the three basic phases of spiritual unfoldment. *Tryptich* is a book to read and reread! Each chapter stands by itself, yet as a part in a vast symphony of revealed values and inspired imagery.
Paper 320pp.   **$9.95**

ASTROLOGICAL ASPECTS:
A Process Oriented Approach
with Leyla Rael Rudhyar
A cyclic and holistic approach to aspects including chapters on retrogradation, rectangular· and triangular aspect patterns, seeing the horoscope intuitively as a whole, Yods, an explanation of the three types of every planetary aspect with examples and practical applications.
Paper 244pp.   **$9.95**

PERSON CENTERED ASTROLOGY

Lucid and inspiring material on the purpose of Astrology in New Age guidance and the difference between an event-oriented approach and a person centered view. Illustrated with complete case studies, concrete examples of the holistic approach in action and practical technique.
Paper 385pp.   **$19.95**

THE LUNATION PROCESS IN ASTROLOGICAL GUIDANCE

Leyla Rael Rudhyar
The only book available on the use of the Progressed Lunation Cycle as a tool in process oriented Life Interpretation. The technique, theory, and phases are explained in detail with several whole life case histories to illustrate the use of this valuable technique.
Paper 62pp.   **$3.95**

TILLING THE SOUL
**An Exciting New Approach to
Growing Consciousness**
Wingate
A truly unusual book, produced and designed to allow new concepts to emerge
while "experiencing" reading it. The introduction gives the essence of this growth
book: "No one has ever called me a Perfect
Master. Nor do I go around claiming to be
Enlightened. But I've studied with good
teachers. I've done my homework. I practice
what I teach. And I'm growing. In *Tilling The
Soul*, I share with you my growth practices
and the basic tools I use, along with some of
the fruits of my gardening. Perhaps these
tools and these practices of mine will help
you in cultivating the garden of your own
consciousness, as they have already helped
me and many others who have studied with
me at the Communion of Souls. "We are
standing on the threshold of a wondrous New
Age, the Age Of The Soul. No longer will we
seek our truths and realizations outside ourselves, where we have been looking so unsuc-
cessfully for so many lifetimes. "In the New
Age of Soul we will find them deep within
ourselves, and we will find our happiness and
our fulfillment there also." In other words,
we will stop looking in all the wrong places
and chasing all the wrong rainbows. Instead
we will seek first Soul Consciousness, secure
in the knowing that all else will inevitably
follow. We will become "TILLERS OF THE
SOUL."
Paper 220pp. $9.95

CELESTIAL PSYCHOLOGY
Doris Hebel
A comprehensive investigation of planetary
energies and their effect on human consciousness, transcending conventional
astrological interpretation and delineation.
An in-depth blend of Astrology and Psychology encompassing both the esoteric and ex-
oteric levels of planetary manifestation in
human behavior and experience. Included
are numerous mental, emotional, physical
and spiritual remedial techniques designed
to assist in dealing with the implications and
complexes inherent in specific planetary
combinations.
$8.95

SILVER DENTAL FILLINGS:
The Toxic Timebomb
Sam Ziff
A significant and shocking exposé of one of
the greatest health dangers of our time. The
amalgam used to fill teeth is 40 to 50 per cent
Mercury. It is explained in this book how it
migrates from the teeth into the body affect-
ing our overall health in a dramatic manner.
This groundbreaking book includes:

  Mercury in medicine and dentistry
  The history of mercury in medicine
  The arguments for and against
  Do we really have electricity in our
     mouths?
  Measurement of Mercury in the urine
  Mercury in the body, where does it go?
  How long does it stay?
  Does Mercury cause any changes in our
     tissues and organs?
  Fantasy or fact, does Mercury cause psy-
     chiatric and behavioral changes?
  Micromercurialism, signs and symptoms

This book is written in a clear straightforward
manner, ideal for the layman and professional, who wants to become aware of the
body of information currently available on
Mercury toxicity. Then, informed, each individual can draw their own conclusions.
Paper 168pp. $8.95

TAOIST SECRETS OF LOVE—
CULTIVATING MALE SEXUAL ENERGY
Mantak Chia
The ancient sexual secrets of the Taoist sages
enable men to conserve and transform sexual
energy through its circulation in the Micro-
cosmic Orbit, invigorating and rejuvenating
the body's vital functions. Hidden for cen-
turies, these esoteric techniques and principles make the process of linking sexual
energy and transcendent states of consciousness accessible to the reader.
Paper 285pp. $10.95

AURORA PRESS

Aurora Press is devoted to pioneering books that catalyze personal growth, balance and transformation. Aurora makes available in a digestible format, an innovative synthesis of ancient wisdom with twentieth century resources, integrating esoteric knowledge and daily life.

Recent titles include:

COMING HOME
Deborah Duda

CRYSTAL ENLIGHTENMENT
Katrina Raphaell

CRYSTAL HEALING
Katrina Raphaell

SILVER DENTAL FILLINGS • THE TOXIC TIMEBOMB
Sam Ziff

AWAKEN HEALING ENERGY THROUGH THE TAO
Mantak Chia

TAOIST SECRETS OF LOVE
Mantak Chia

THE LUNATION CYCLE
Dane Rudhyar

SELF HEALING, YOGA AND DESTINY
Elisabeth Haich

For a complete catalog write:

AURORA PRESS
P.O. BOX 573
SANTA FE NEW MEXICO 87504
(505) 989-9804